Secret Places of the Goddess
Contacting the Earth Spirit

By Philip Heselton

Secret Places of the Goddess
Contacting the Earth Spirit

©1995 Philip Heselton

ISBN 1 898307 40 7

ALL RIGHTS RESERVED

No part of this publication may be reproduced, stored in a retrieval system or transmitted in any form or by any means, electronic, mechanical, photocopying, scanning, recording or otherwise without the prior written permission of the author and the publisher.

Cover design by Daryth Bastin
Cover Illustration by Sue Mason

Published by:

Capall Bann Publishing
Freshfields
Chieveley
Berks
RG20 8TF

For Jane who inspired in me the urge to write this volume

For Hilary who has been my companion in the secret places

And for Owen and Aidan in the hope that they may find those secret places for themselves

By the same author:
Skyways and Landmarks Revisited (with Jimmy Goddard and Baines) [1985]
Earth Mysteries - An Exploratory Introduction (with Brian Larkman) [1985]
Tony Wedd - New Age Pioneer [1986]
The Elements of Earth Mysteries [1991]

CONTENTS

FOREWORD AND ACKNOWLEDGEMENTS	1
CHAPTER 1 THE MAGIC OF PLACE	3
CHAPTER 2 THE EARTH SPIRIT	13
CHAPTER 3 THE WILD WOOD	27
The Glade in the Thicket	30
Sacred Groves	38
Forgotten Land - the Boundary between the Worlds	49
CHAPTER 4 THE BODY OF THE EARTH GODDESS	53
CHAPTER 5 THE WATERS OF LIFE	65
Sacred Springs	65
Streams and Waterfalls	70
Ponds - Mirrors of Magic	73
The Seashore	80
CHAPTER 6 SPIRIT PATHS TO HOLY HILLS	84
CHAPTER 7 FINDING OUR PLACE	93
CHAPTER 8 ENTERING THE PRESENCE	108
Access	110
Sites for All Seasons	116
Boundaries, Gateways and Guardians	118
CHAPTER 9 INBREATH - EXPERIENCING THE SACRED SPACE	131
Scent	135
Taste	139
Feeling	140
Sound	142
Light	144
Psyche	146
CHAPTER OUTBREATH - RESPONDING TO THE SPIRIT	153
Tending the Site	155
Between the Worlds: Casting the Circle	161
Relating to the Landscape	164
The Wheel of the Year	165

i

The Moods of the Earth and Sky	167
Words, Calls and Cries	168
CHAPTER 11 EMBRACING THE SITE	171
The Use of Working Tools	179
Giving and Taking	184
Acting Spontaneously	185
Practical Considerations	187
Feeling the Response	188
ENDWORDS	191
FURTHER READING	193
REFERENCES	194

FOREWORD AND ACKNOWLEDGEMENTS

The idea for this book arose initially from a desire to help pagans and others to seek inspiration in the landscape which is, as I describe it, the environment of the Goddess.

I hope it will be both a practical and evocative guide to help people to get closer to the landscape in their pagan activities, and encountering the Goddess and the God in their own domain. I suggest ways this might happen.

Even when we live in the countryside, most of us are urban dwellers in terms of our life-style, and we may need some help to achieve what, for those of previous generations - practitioners of the traditional Craft - was just natural and right.

I have quoted extensively from pagan writers and others because it was important to me that the book had a wider base than just my own experiences. I hope that through these accounts, which in many cases are highly personal, you will gain some emotional understanding of what is going on.

I could never have written this book without the help and encouragement of numerous friends who have been very positive about the whole project:

Karen and Paul Atkin, Elizabeth Baker, John Billingsley, Hilary Byers, Linda Carr, Amanda Class, Mériém and Alastair Clay-Egerton, Andrew Collins, Charla and Paul Devereux, Jane and Bob Dickinson, Roy Dresser, Audrey Dunne, Frank Earp, Ben Fernee, Alec Gill, Jimmy Goddard, James Hamilton, Jeremy Harte, Joan and Kenneth Heselton, Nigel and Susan Heselton, Penny Hill, Michael Howard, Louise Jennings, Brian Larkman, Brian McCoy, John Merron, John Michell, Jonathan Mullard, James Pengelly, Nigel Pennick, Gentian Rahtz, Lydia Rain, Eileen Roche, Jill Smith, Kim Taplin, Ian Taylor, Bob Trubshaw, Kay Watkins, Edna Whelan, Samantha White and Derrick and Anthea Wilbie-Chalk.

In particular, I would like to thank Mériém Clay-Egerton and Kay Watkins for permission to quote from unpublished manuscripts; Jill Smith for permission to reproduce her poem "Chanctonbury Rings" and Bob Dickinson for permission to include his poem about the Devil's Pulpit.

CHAPTER 1

THE MAGIC OF PLACE

Seeking and finding the numinous - the magical - at special secret places in our surroundings appears to be such a universal experience that it seems almost archetypal by nature. The wisdom of the Earth, the magic of place, are vital for our survival as healthy and sensitive individuals.

My early memories include playing in a small patch of woodland going by the name of "The Jungle". Here one could escape, for a time at least, from the tidiness of suburbia. It was an overgrown triangle of land, consisting primarily of elder, ash and thorn, but it was a gateway to another world - an echo of a wilder nature welling up from within the depths of my being, where one could experience vivid sunsets, the wind in a clump of nearby pines and birds flying in formation, both black against the evening sky, opening up the memory of some other place and time for a moment that seemed to last for ever. It fulfilled a need that has remained constant in all the intervening years - somewhere I could go to be on my own and think.

I became strongly aware of this need when I first went camping with the local scout troop on Bredon Hill in Worcestershire. I enjoyed myself, but, towards the evening of the second day, was getting increasingly tense and felt very strange. Suddenly, I felt the strong urge to leave the others and made straight for a clump of tall gorse bushes. Ignoring the prickles, I plunged straight in and found myself in a small clearing surrounded by bushes. I stood very still. I could still hear the others' chatter some distance away but I was on my own. Suddenly, I realised: I had not been on my own for a single moment of the previous 24 hours and I needed to be. I felt the anxiety and tension drain away as I stood there: it only needed a few minutes and I was able to return fully refreshed. It was a lesson that has stayed with me.

In my childhood we used to go for country holidays, often hiring a caravan placed in the corner of a field or farmyard and my first act on arriving was always to go out for a walk, to find 'my place' for the fortnight. It may have been a clump of old beech trees, a natural rock hollow on top of a hill, or a spreading oak tree on the edge of an ancient wood.

On one occasion, it was just the corner of a field, a little lower than the rest, so that my view was limited to the front by the rising ground and to the rear by two large hawthorn hedges, meeting at the corner. My world, for that time, was limited by these boundaries - it felt secure. The 'headland' - that narrow belt of grass between the hedge and the cultivated field - widened at the corner to provide a small sheltered and protected spot for me to stand close to the hedge - a sacred spot I visited several times a day during the time I was there.

These special places have all remained in my memory over the years, together with the feelings, ideas and experiences which I had there - elusive, not to be taken for granted but, when they happen, memorable, significant and joyous.

Talking with others and reading the available literature have made it clear to me that many people's deepest experiences, whether they be attaining 'cosmic consciousness', having a flow of poetic inspiration or making love, take place at particular spots in the landscape. This has happened in other people's experience sufficiently often for me to begin to feel that some archetypal principle was involved - that of re-integration with the Earth of which we are a part.

There is certainly in many a growing awareness of the land and of its character and cycles. It has resulted in the upsurge of interest in what have come to be known as "green" issues, of increased ecological awareness and of membership of such groups as Friends of the Earth. I feel this is a natural result of what we might see as a deep inner longing for the Earth.

A complementary result has been a resurgence of what has been called "green spirituality" - the necessity for a central place to be accorded to an ecological approach in religious practice and philosophy. Pagan religions, with their strong tradition that we are a part of the Earth, have as a consequence come into greater prominence in recent years. In a variety of forms, paganism exists throughout the world: Australian aborigine beliefs and practices, the native American tradition, as well as witchcraft and Druidism, can all be encompassed within its cloak and, whilst varied in their particular expression, have in common their close link with and reverence for the Earth and special places in the landscape.

I started to call myself pagan a few years ago because that description seemed to fall happily in with the sort of experiences which I was having. This is no rigid or exclusive religious belief or doctrine, however, and my whole emphasis is on an inclusive paganism, where every act or feeling which leads towards the realisation of our unity with the rest of Nature is pagan in essence.

The Bull Rock - guardian of a nearby cave

What I don't want to do is to separate it out, making it seem something that only a minority might aspire to. The essential message in this book is that potentially paganism can suffuse all of life.

I am reminded of Colin Ward's book "*Anarchy in Action*"[86]. In it he tries to show that anarchism is not some obscure and impractical political philosophy, and that people are already acting in anarchist ways in their everyday lives and ordinary activities. In other words, that an anarchist, i.e. non-coercive, approach can be discerned in many ordinary day-to-day contacts between people going about their daily lives.

I try to do the same for paganism (which I therefore spell with a small "p") showing how each time we have the urge to go out for a picnic in the countryside, walk through the woods or enjoy the crescent moon in the evening sky, we are engaged in pagan activities, even if we don't call it that. Looked at in this way, paganism is the one religion you don't have to teach: children are naturally pagan - they are aware of being a part of Nature and will naturally express this in many different ways.

So, this book is for everyone who has felt some urge to go out and rest for a few minutes under a spreading oak tree, feeling its healing spirit enter and strengthen them. My purpose has been to encourage the reader out into the countryside (and the 'unofficial countryside' hidden in our towns and cities) to find those locations which are special to you and where you can start to achieve that reintegration with what has been called by some the Earth Spirit and by others the Earth Goddess.

There are many reasons for wanting to find a special place - perhaps for meditation, to get inspiration for writing, to sort out some problems, for prayer or magical working.

The book starts by focusing on what John Michell has called the Earth Spirit[53] - how it can be felt and in what sort of places it can be found.

I then suggest practical steps towards finding and getting to know those Secret Places of the Goddess, together with actions you might take towards that magical experience of unity which is so delicate that no rigid ritual can guarantee success.

I stress throughout the book the Taoist principle of direct experience: words so often get in the way and, because of this, it is often difficult to see, or experience, what is actually there. I have certainly found this in writing and use terms such as special or secret place, spot, site and location interchangeably, as I do the Earth Spirit, the Life Force, the Goddess and the God, the Old Ones and the Spirit of the Place. Ultimately it doesn't matter, since the experience is beyond words and it is only by going beyond the words that the reality can be experienced. Much of the book is thus a record of experiences at places in the landscape.

However, I wanted this book to be more than just my own ideas, so I have asked my friends for their own experiences of sites and locations special to them. I also looked extensively through back issues of numerous pagan and earth mysteries magazines for articles that expressed something of that direct experience at places in the landscape that I was looking for.

My first impression was how few articles there were which had material I could use. Most were heavily biased towards the intellectual but from this massive thicket there shone a few outstanding pieces that made my trawl through the material worthwhile.

So, what is calling us? Why do we feel the need to go out into the landscape? At the most fundamental level, that is the domain of the Goddess and if we want to meet her, we have to go where we can find her. When I am away from people, usually under a tree, I (and I know from speaking to others that I am far from being alone) can in some strange way open up whilst my rhythms slow down and my aura expands. Although encompassing a lot more than that, it involves "long term thinking", which is a description which has been applied to meditation. Writing in a totally different context, Anna Thomas' description of sharing a meal with friends has something of the same quality:

> *"We've all been to perfect dinner parties - the ones where the guests enjoy one another, the conversation is good, each course pleases the palate and is exquisitely timed, time itself vanishes, and only harmonious presence flows on effortlessly - until it all is suddenly over. The guests go home and the beautiful ruin of a table remains. Friendships bloom at such dinners, optimism is restored, and one begins to notice the extraordinary colour of the wine. The chemistry of such a gathering is elusive."*[80]

When I am in a magical spot in the landscape my sense of my own worth is strengthened, things are put into perspective and, most special of all, there is an increase in sensitivity at all levels from awareness of my immediate physical environment to becoming more open to the real needs of my friends and acquaintances.

As an example of this, one of William Morris' best-known political essays is entitled "Under an Elm Tree"[58]. It starts with a very vivid description of the countryside in midsummer, with Morris resting in the shadow of a roadside elm. The very beauty of the countryside leads him on to the need to protect it from such threats as commercialisation.

So, seeking out and experiencing that special quality that can be found need be no escapism from the reality of everyday life. At most, perhaps, it is a temporary escape, so we can be filled with the spirit which can permeate that life, so that right decisions are made and actions taken.

One of the features which distinguish paganism is that it has its roots firmly in the land. Whilst most religions have their sacred sites, the significance which the landscape has for pagans is unique - every tree, stone and spring are in some way special, and are representative of the Goddess. Pagans meet the Goddess in her own domain and the consequence of this is that they tend to perform their rituals in the landscape rather than build artificial temples and churches. This is a positive statement about our relationship with the land, which Keith Symes expresses movingly:

> *"We already have temples to the Goddess. By every running stream, at the place where three or four paths meet, by standing stone and ancient circle, in woodland glen; these are the "temples" built by nature or ancient man where we can commune with the Life Force.*
> *The ceilings of these natural temples is the sky, awash with summer blueness or sparkling with a million stars. The walls are the trees of oak, ash, rowan, birch and willow which are sacred to the Old Gods. The floor is the green grass scattered with wild flowers and carpeted with the dry leaves of autumn's dying breath. Surely we have no need of any other temples than the ones provided by Mother Nature herself.""*

In practical terms, of course, this not only frees us from the considerable costs which a permanent building implies, but also increases enormously the number of places which can be used for ritual and other purposes, such places being the subject of this book.

Paganism has all the characteristics of what Joseph Campbell has called a 'Type I' religion. He has classified the religions of the world into two basic types. The older religions, including Hinduism, Buddhism and Taoism, see the universe in a similar way to pagans, holding that the universe and time are cyclical, that ultimately there is no distinction between ourselves and the rest of the universe, that consciousness and spirit are diffused throughout the universe and that we can experience the Divine directly.[8]

Indeed, one of the clearest expressions of paganism is to be found in Taoism and Zen, both of which originate in the Far East. In essence they get beyond intellectualising and lead us back to direct experience of the universe. This is exactly the same message that will be found in any pagan tradition anywhere in the world.

To be consistent with this, therefore, I shouldn't be writing a book at all but, as a wise teacher once said, should be taking you by the hand and walking with you through the nearest wood. My excuse and hope is that this book will be a partial substitute for that walk.

I am actually suggesting a very simple and natural process. You are probably doing it anyway and it may involve little more than walking to a nearby tree and standing under it for a few minutes. My intention is to encourage those who have so far only performed rituals in the comfort of their sitting room to venture forth into the vast open spaces and wild woods which are the realm of the Goddess and the God, and to seek out the hidden natural spring or sacred oaken grove.

It may sometimes be awkward and uncomfortable but the benefits outweigh this many times.

For my own part, the ecstasy of standing skyclad in a sacred beech grove at midnight under a Full Moon, with the wind making wild music in the branches and enveloping one's whole body, hearing the flow of water from the natural spring at one's feet and hearing the echo of the owls crying in the distance - this is something so special and wonderful that it cannot ever be fully expressed in words. All I can hope is that you will be able to discern some faint reflection of the reality of the experience and be inspired to try it for yourself.

CHAPTER 2

THE EARTH SPIRIT

In seeking out those special numinous places, we are taking a journey towards what Nigel Pennick has called the Anima Loci. He says:

> "As human beings, we are rooted in the Earth, but urban civilization is very effective in obscuring the fact. Most people appear to be unaware of it. Traditional wisdom recognizes our relationship with subtle qualities in the land. This is expressed in the relationship between each individual and the land: it manifests its spiritual nature in different places by differing spiritual qualities. We can have a personal spiritual relationship to these qualities.
>
> In simple terms, these experiences can be described as our personal relationships to the goddess of the landscape, which is Mother Earth in her local form. From the 18th century, this has been described as the Genius Loci (spirit of the place), but it can be described better as the Anima Loci (place soul). It can be experienced by anyone anywhere, and it is essentially personal and ineffable."[63]

One of the characteristics of Joseph Campbell's 'Type I' religions is an acceptance that the whole of existence is, at root, a unity. That not only is everything in the universe connected to everything else, but that, at the most fundamental level, everything is one.

Writing about these older spiritual traditions, Fritjof Capra, the physicist, says:

> *"Although [they] differ in many details, their view of the world is essentially the same. It is a view which is based on mystical experience - on a direct non-intellectual experience of reality - and this experience has a number of fundamental characteristics which are independent of the mystic's geographical, historical, or cultural background. ... The most important characteristic of the Eastern world view - one could almost say the essence of it - is the awareness of the unity and mutual interrelation of all things and events, the experience of all phenomena in the world as manifestations of a basic oneness. All things are seen as interdependent and inseparable parts of this cosmic whole; as different manifestations of the same ultimate reality. The Eastern traditions constantly refer to this ultimate, indivisible reality which manifests itself in all things, and of which all things are parts."*[9]

Such a world view is not just "Eastern" but an integral part of pagan religions from all parts of the world. As Capra emphasises, it is not primarily a theoretical concept, but a practical one, grounded in experience - the experience which has been known by many names over the years but which, since the publication of an influential book of that title by R.M. Bucke in 1901, has become known as Cosmic Consciousness.

Bucke found that people from widely differing backgrounds and cultures described certain striking and unusual experiences in remarkably similar ways, principal among them being the knowledge that the individual was an integral part of the whole. By 'cosmic consciousness' he meant being in a certain state of mind/spirit which had certain characteristics, constantly repeated in the cases he studied - being vividly aware of "the life and order of the universe", having "an intellectual enlightenment or illumination", feeling "elevation, elation and joyousness" and attaining a consciousness that we "have eternal life".[6]

Clearly, there are profound implications if we take such experiences and corresponding world view seriously. Not least, they provide a framework into which we can fit all the various forms of psychic phenomena. If, at the most fundamental level, the whole universe is a unity, then clearly the process underlying such things as telepathy, clairvoyance etc. becomes clear. It also enables the processes behind magical working to be better understood.

Our everyday experience, however, is not so much the underlying unity but the diversity of life. To quote Capra again:

> *"In ordinary life, we are not aware of this unity of all things, but divide the world into separate objects and events. This division is, of course, useful and necessary to cope with our everyday environment, but it is not a fundamental feature of reality. It is an abstraction devised by our discriminating and categorizing intellect."*[9]

Things appear different and distinct from each other and thus we can recognise them, seeing ourselves, for example, as separate from our environment. At the ultimate level, this is an illusion, what Alan Watts called the myth of the skin-encapsulated ego, but it enables us to go about our daily lives.

By training, I am a geographer. Now it is generally agreed that geography is about place - what makes up the character of a place and how places differ from each other. In practice, this can be a very complex and subtle interaction of factors, but it comes down to attempting to explain why places are distinct - in other words, how we know where we are.

The sort of geography which is taught in schools and universities concerns itself with the effect of the varying rock strata on the landscape, soil, vegetation, settlement pattern, etc. By contrast, what I want to look at is what we might call 'Subtle Geography', by recognising the existence of variations in the less tangible factors that make up a landscape. Mystics, shamans and others who are in touch with the deeper parts of themselves, which links with everything else, have always been sensitive to such subtle distinctions. Carmen Blacker gives a practical example of this:

> *"Mr Mizoguchi could also see through his faculty of gantsu [clairvoyance] the presence of a benign numen in certain trees and rocks. In the autumn of 1963 he kindly guided me to the summit of Mt Miwa, and as we walked up the path through the forest I noticed that certain cryptomeria trees and rocks wore the girdle of straw rope which, like a sacramental belt or collar, marks objects imbued with a numinous presence. To me these trees and stones appeared indistinguishable from those without the straw girdle. From a certain pile of stones, for example, two had been favoured by the straw rope, whereas the rest were bare. How was it possible, I asked Mr Mizoguchi, to tell which trees and stones were*

numinous and which were not. Entirely by the faculty of gantsu, was his reply. Those who had developed this faculty through the practice of austerities could see the deity inhering in the stone or tree."[5]

This distinguishing between objects, spots and places, apparently identical to all outward appearances, by means of a sensitivity to some hidden property which some of them possess, is a recognition of that Spirit of Place which is the subject of this book. This may not be a conscious recognition. Indeed, in most of us it probably remains deeply buried. At some level, however, it is present and its effects can be seen at any popular 'beauty spot' on a sunny Sunday afternoon in summer.

The sort of countryside that people most like to visit seems to be "scenic attractions" like the Lake District (and indeed all the National Parks and Areas of Outstanding Natural Beauty), the New Forest and more specific spots like Cheddar Gorge, the Wye Valley and so on. Features such as mountains and hills, rock outcrops, steep-sided valleys, waterfalls and lakes, old woodland, are characteristic of such places. John Michell has referred to them as being centres of the Earth Spirit and captures the "feel" of what he is referring to in the following passage:

"Rocks, trees, mountains, wells and springs were recognized as receptacles for spirit, displaying in season their various properties, fertilizing, therapeutic and oracular. ... Characteristic of the earth spirit, and in accordance with its feminine nature, is its tendency to withdraw, to decline within the earth's dark recesses. ... Attempts to fix nature's volatile principle will always be made; and the spirit may for a time accept the ways imposed on it by human nature in its material aspect.

> *But sooner or later it will prefer its own ways, and will take them, whatever obstacles are put in its path. Behind this animated current is the Mystery, hinted at in the catacombs of Eleusis, that may not fully be comprehended within the natural limits of human experience."*[53]

What we are encountering is something subtle, elusive, magical. This is in its nature. We cannot understand it with our rational minds. It is best just to acknowledge it as a living experience, flowing with its characteristic moods, being flexible and sensitive, recognising that at heart the Earth Spirit is one of the manifestations of the Goddess. Ultimately, the Earth Spirit is something beyond normal everyday reality. It is a manifestation of the Otherworld - the life-blood of the Earth Goddess - and only if we are in tune with her and her rhythms can we experience her spirit at those special secret places and times when she chooses to reveal herself to us.

Some have attempted to detect the presence of the Earth Spirit with dowsing rods and scientific instruments. But the emphasis of this book is on direct experience, recognising and acknowledging the Earth Spirit as the living presence of the Goddess - we may gradually get to know certain aspects of her being but this can only happen if we approach her in an attitude of humility, recognising that we approach her on her own terms.

Anyone who has experienced it first-hand knows without doubt that there is something there, and the phrase 'Earth Spirit' is probably a good one to use when referring to it, provided we are aware that we and the landscape are living beings, responding to the cycles of the universe and that what we may experience on one occasion may be very different from what someone else experiences on another.

Ultimately, the important thing is not to define the Earth Spirit, but to experience it.

Just as in a relationship with another person, recognition of the Earth Spirit is something we should never take for granted. The most we can do is to set up the circumstances that seem favourable to its manifestation.

How might we recognise the presence of the Earth Spirit? The first point to make is that this occurs as an interaction between ourselves and our environment at a particular moment in time, each of which is part of a fluctuating cycle. So the particular combination of circumstances at any moment never repeats itself - each experience is unique. It is important to remember this before attempting to compare your experience with that of anyone else - they are bound to be different! It is the same as the old story of the blind men feeling different parts of the elephant and then arguing as to what the elephant was like. The experiences that people have when in the presence of the Earth Spirit are varied. It is a living manifestation of the Earth Goddess and can never be confined to a formula.

Some have experienced physical effects, such as tingling in the hands or other parts of the body, "head-hum" or a feeling of disorientation. Others have had their psychic sense magnified and perhaps seen evidence of nature spirits or other beings on the edge of normal perception. But the strongest or most archetypal experience is that which is most difficult to define in words - it is the awareness of the presence of the Goddess. It has been the objective of ritual such as that of Drawing Down the Moon and, when it occurs, it is truly beyond words.

And perhaps it is quite in order not to know exactly what we are dealing with. We cannot demand the presence of the Goddess. On the contrary, we have to go to her special places in the landscape and get to know some of her ways. Then, if we are fortunate and she smiles on us, we may experience the Earth Spirit in its fullness.

The archaeologist and dowser Tom Lethbridge detected by dowsing and in other ways what he called the earth's "force field" and found it concentrated in certain locations, where he referred to it as a "static field":

> *"All we need to notice is that these static fields are to be found in connection with such things as waterfalls, springs and streams, or woods and trees, deserts and moorlands and mountains. This is extremely important to anyone who is interested in mythology. For these are just the places which were peopled with nymphs and spirits by the peoples of the ancient world and by simple modern ones. These nymphs and spirits must be the result of observation by people at what is known, somewhat contemptuously, as a primitive level of culture. Such people are far more observant than the bulk of the population today. ... The things which I believe they notice are, amongst others of course, the static fields at these particular places. They also observe the movements of beast and bird and the signs which indicate these movements."*[48]

These nymphs which he drew attention to were said to inhabit the landscape of the classical world - 'naiads' living in waterfalls, springs and streams, 'dryads' in trees and woods, 'oreads' in mountains and deserts, and 'nereids' in the sea. He came to the conclusion that some people could perceive these nymphs when their own aura, in a state of emotional arousal, interacted with the "force field" of the place.

Michell refers to "rocks, trees, mountains, wells and springs"; Lethbridge to waterfalls, springs, streams, trees, woods, mountains, deserts and the sea. This strong overlap gives us a clue as to some of the places where the Earth Spirit might be found. And these two writers are not alone - there are many references to such a spirit inhabiting the landscape from the most ancient times to the present day.

Some of the most vivid accounts come from the Australian aborigine and native American traditions. The problem in the past is that those who have written about these traditions did not have the words for the concepts that were being expressed. However, it is now quite clear that such peoples were and remain, very sensitive to the living nature of their environment, including those subtle distinctions that we generally would not notice. The spirit world and its geography is a very real and immediate thing to them, in a way that was true with rural dwellers in our own landscape in former years but which has now been largely lost.

The Chinese called it ch'i, the yogis of India referred to prana; in the Northern Tradition it was called önd and wouivre; the mediaeval alchemists referred to it as munia and the Hawaiian kahunas as mana. Mesmer knew it as animal magnetism, von Reichenbach as odyle and, in the present century, Wilhelm Reich worked extensively on orgone energy. These are only a small proportion of the guises in which the Earth Spirit has been known, but they are remarkably consistent in the characteristics which they ascribe to it.

The existence of such a similar concept in so many cultures, distant from each other in time, space and sophistication, points to the existence of an archetypal principle which must have significance in our lives and activities, regardless of whether it has a corresponding physical reality.

As my emphasis in this book is on personal experience, of what we feel at certain places and how that can help us to come closer to the Earth Goddess, those traditions which have an element of personal experience may well provide a valuable clue.

One tradition is provided by the folklore and legend attached to places in the landscape. If we look at such stories, it is remarkable how they tend to be associated with just the sort of sites referred to by Michell and Lethbridge. But it is important to be clear what sort of thing we are dealing with when looking at folklore. It is likely to be based on handed-down and elaborated reports of something which may once have been experienced. So the stories need to be interpreted. The persistence, however, with which legend is attached to certain specific sites and not to others superficially similar suggests an origin based on experience rather than total invention.

In my own area, stones and springs seem to be the particular sites to which folk tales have been attached. The Holy Well at Atwick, for example, which is now more of a rushy pool, is said to be haunted by the ghost of a woman. High up on the Wolds, a long way from the nearest habitation, and hidden from the nearby road, are the Fairy Stones. They are a magical place, full of some strange power, and there are legends attached to them, including one which states that if a young man were to go up there at midnight of the Full Moon, he will see his love. Fairies are also to be seen at this time, according to legend. And these can be repeated many hundreds of times throughout the land.

The point to note is that the tales relate to an experience of some presence (in one case interpreted as a ghost, in the other as fairies) at a special place in the landscape.

One of the first things one realises when studying geography is the extent to which the landscape, and certainly the English landscape, is the result of the interaction between people and natural forces. The main emphasis in this book is on the natural sites in the landscape - springs, rock outcrops, hilltops, for example, but all have been affected by human action to some extent, some more obviously than others. No site is 100% "natural" and no site in the countryside is completely artificial. It would be true to say that our landscape is an intermingling of the two. We can say that where people have acted, whether consciously or not, in accord with the rhythms of the universe they have helped to create something which is in harmony with the underlying character of a place - its spirit. The form created will as a result be part of the landscape and will look right.

Most of us have experienced those places where the artificial elements in the landscape enhance its character in a subtle way. They may not be overly impressive or obvious features. I am thinking here of such things as the line of a trackway over an undulating landscape, or the position of a small dewpond, field-gate or field-corner clump. Such incidental or forgotten features add to the significance of the landscape.

The locations in which ancient stone circles, standing stones, "burial chambers" and mounds are placed often say something very powerful about how the ancient people related to the landscape. Visiting such ancient spots, you will learn as much about the landscape as you will about the feature itself.

Delphi, one of the most sacred centres in Greece, originated in ancient times as a fissure in the ground from which vapours emanated. These had the quality of causing anyone who inhaled them to enter into a form of trance.

Lourdes, in south-west France, has become a major centre of pilgrimage and healing. Its origins lie in a grotto or cave from which a spring flowed. A 14-year old girl, Bernadette Soubirous, in what appears to have been an altered state of consciousness, saw something white in the grotto, which she described initially as 'that thing' and subsequently as a young girl. Perhaps because of the culture in which she lived, this was soon interpreted as a vision of the Virgin Mary.

In both of these examples, we can see that the sacred centre started as a natural feature in the landscape which in certain circumstances was able to induce in individuals powers of vision and prophecy, what we might today categorise as an altered state of consciousness.

Many have been inspired by those places where the Earth Spirit can be encountered, not least those writers, poets, artists and composers who have been able to express their response in creative ways.

Landscape and special places within it have inspired so many to creative action that a study of this really invites a book in its own right. The Lake Poets (Wordsworth, Coleridge and Southey), John Clare, William Barnes, Thomas Hardy and John Cowper Powys are just a very few of those who gained inspiration from, and wrote about, special places in the landscape.

Tennyson used to sit for hours beside Black Hill Spring near his home in Lincolnshire, a beautiful and isolated spot where a stream flows out from the hillside in a sheltered cove.

The composer, Edward Elgar, seemed to obtain much of his inspiration from places in the landscape:

"... *Elgar was still the lover of solitary paths; the Malvern Hills beckoned constantly, even in the heart of London's theatreland (which he also loved). Perhaps, in his way, he was indeed something of a mystic. He spoke repeatedly of hearing songs and sounds that others didn't. 'Music is in the air all around you,' he used to say, 'Music is written on the skies.' As a boy he was as one who lived in two worlds: as a man and a composer he wrote music that reached out to bridge the mysterious gap between.*"[65]

Special places in the landscape can also form the subject matter of literary works. Alan Richardson has said of "*The Sea Priestess*" by Dion Fortune, "It is the finest occult novel ever written. No one before or since has come remotely close to matching it."[68] Many of her novels have, as an integral part of their theme, the landscape and the importance of special sites within it. "*The Sea Priestess*" has a marshland setting adjacent to the sea, with rivers and former rivercourses, hills rising up out of the marsh, a rocky headland and a cave high up on a cliff. All these have significance in the story, but above all it is the sea and its moon-influenced tides, which is central.

"*The Goat-Foot God*" is set in the chalk hills beyond the built-up confines of London. It climaxes in a rite to invoke Pan, which takes place within an ancient yew grove, which is discovered at the appropriate time:

"*They had never explored the wood very thoroughly because it was beset with brambles, but Hugh, taking giant's strides, lifted his long bare legs over these and reached its shade, hoping to find some sort of cover among the undergrowth.*

He pushed on, finding it easier going now that the shade made the growth scanty, and saw ahead of him a dense mass of dark foliage among red-brown trunks. This looked hopeful, and he headed towards it, to find a close-set belt of yews blocking his path. The yew is a long-lived, slow-growing tree, and from the girth of these he judged they must be pretty ancient, and with a sudden quickening of heart-beat, wondered whether they dated from Ambrosius' day, and if so, why they had been planted?

He ducked under the low-hanging outer branches, and with some difficulty forced his way through, to come out into a little open glade entirely surrounded by yews. Here was the very privacy he desired! He took stock of his surroundings while he picked the yew-needles out of his hair and shirt-collar."[28]

Writing about art, and poetry in particular, Kim Taplin states:

"It in some way participates in the renewing, sustaining power of the earth itself. Part of poetry's function is the reminding us, magically, what is our relationship to the earth. Robert Graves went so far as to suggest, in The White Goddess (1948), that it was its sole true function."[78]

In this chapter I have deliberately not defined the Earth Spirit too closely. It is magical and it can come upon us at unexpected times and places. We cannot take it for granted. It is the aura of the Goddess and by attuning ourselves with it and with her we can realise our place in the Earth and the responsibility that this implies.

CHAPTER 3

THE WILD WOOD

Historians have a well-known technique for finding out what people did: they look at what was forbidden. I remember, for example, going into a pub recently which had a notice displayed saying something like "Shirts must be worn at all times". From this, it was easy to work out that formerly there must have been the practice of entering without a shirt and that this had for some reason earned the landlord's disapproval! The same applies in more distant times. Vivianne Crowley gives some examples of early edicts:

> *"In AD 959 the Ecclesiastical Canon of King Edgar forbade well worship, man worship, spells and consorting with trees and stones. Similarly King Cnut later forbade worshipping Pagan Gods; Pagan practices with wells, stones and trees; and the love of witchcraft. These pronouncements are useful in that they tell us something about the religious practices of Paganism at the time."[18]*

So, when we note that the early Christians forbade the worship of stones, trees and springs it is fairly clear that people were in fact doing precisely what was forbidden, or at least frequenting such spots for religious purposes.

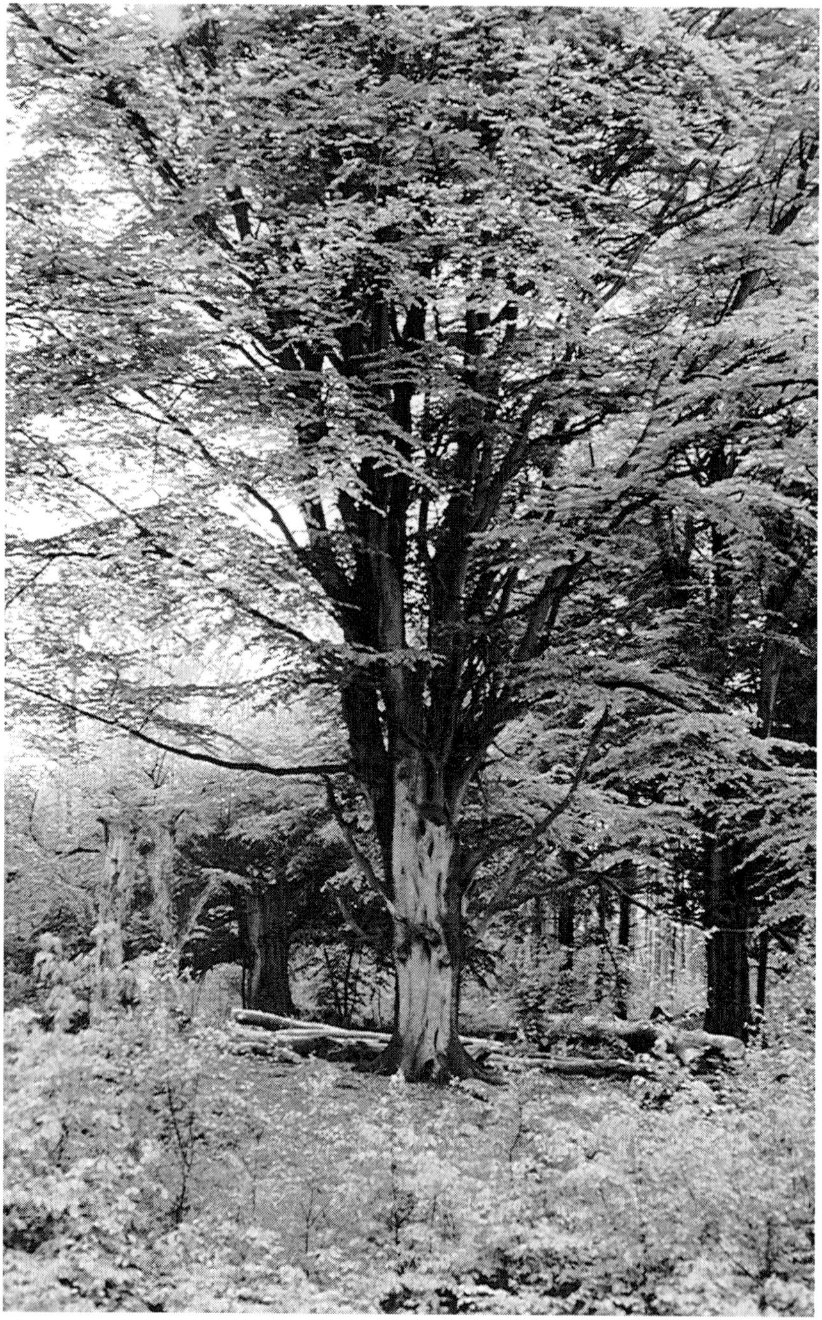

In the next few chapters I set out to cover a broad spectrum of places in the landscape that people find special, with a particular emphasis on the experiences of modern pagans. I have tried to give a feel of these places, in the hope of inspiring those who feel inclined to make the effort to go out to meet the Goddess in the landscape.

In the countryside one is very much aware of the elements and I have used the old classification into Air, Earth, Water and Fire to provide a framework in considering these spots.

Trees represent the element of Air. Except in those very rare moments of absolute calm, they are in constant motion, moved by the air - that invisible but vital ingredient of life.

The wind can also be heard in trees. As Paul Simons says:

"The wind section is probably the biggest component of the weather's orchestra. The sighing sound of the wind blowing through woodlands is made by the vibration of conifer needles or deciduous tree twigs. Changes in the wind modulate the pitch and loudness of the woodlands, and winds gusting strongly through a forest on a mountain slope sometimes produce a roaring sound."[75]

Paul Baines notes that:

"... trees could be attributed to the element of Air, not just on account of the wind blowing through them but because trees are essential to maintaining the oxygen - CO2 balance of the Earth. For this reason they have been referred to as 'the lungs of the Earth'. Note how a deciduous tree in the winter resembles the bronchial 'tree' of the human lungs."[39]

The Glade in the Thicket

If there is one place which can be said to be the archetypal meeting place of present-day pagans and witches, it is the clearing in the wood.

Indeed, the modern revival of interest in witchcraft arose following Gerald Gardner's contact with a traditional group which met in the New Forest. Certainly today, many groups both modern and traditional, continue the practice of performing their rituals in the depths of ancient forests.

Woods have certainly had a profound effect on most of us and been the source of much inspiration. To whatever pagan tradition we might belong, I have found over the years, through reading accounts in books and articles and, above all, through talking to people, that many of us had our first experience of the numinous - that living spirit which lies behind physical form - through walking in the woods. Indeed, this is so universal in those I have talked to that I suspect it to be of a fundamental and archetypal nature.

Certainly in my own case I remember the impatience with which, on childhood visits to my grandmother in Kent, I wanted to go down to the woods. I spent many hours in those woods, past the sentinel oak or following the ancient straight path of Bethersden marble from the churchyard, past a pond with a spring feeding it, over stiles and through gates and into the depths of the wood. I was a pagan even in those days, though I didn't know the word.

Certain woods have that quality which marks out those special places where we can more easily make contact with the Goddess and the God. If we can allow ourselves to feel and act instinctively, we should fairly quickly become aware when this quality or essence is present. Robin Ellis refers to "certain woods and forests" where something infinitely stranger is at work than in "normal" woodland, which he describes as "a sort of creative Otherworld power that seems to be able to interact with the human unconscious". He says :

> *"Such woodlands are comparatively rare, but they represent a tremendous source of spiritual power to us, if we can cope with them! They are not the easiest of places to be in. Firstly, there is the disorientation. You may find yourself walking in a totally different direction to that which you had intended. At times it is almost possible to experience the switch in direction. The deep woods are well defended! If you try to force your way through, you find yourself walking in elaborate circles, even though you are convinced that you are walking in a straight line!"*[26]

This is a point also made by Kati-Ma Koppana:

> *"Anybody at all can go for a walk in the forest, walk quietly and enjoy its beauty, but at a certain point in our journey we must go deeper into the heart of the forest, not merely to see its tall trees, its undergrowth and the path winding forward between it all, but the inner place ... In approaching a forest one must change one's attitude. Forget about being safe in the forest as it can be dangerous. It can trip you up, lose you along the winding paths which might simply wind out again ... The forest may confuse you by putting the same large rock in three different places. Forget safety and replace it with TRUST. If you trust the forest, it will trust you."*[45]

Robin Ellis continues:

> "Once within the deep woods however, you will notice a distinct change in the atmosphere. In this part of the forest you seem to stand in an old, strange, and solemn universe all of its own. Before you can 'go between the worlds', however, your consciousness has to align itself with that of the Wildwood! What happens is that the wood begins to haunt you. Trees seem to move by themselves; the wood becomes preternaturally dark; strange, disturbing sounds are heard from various directions; at night there are strange lights seen glowing in the darkness."[26]

He goes on to write about the uncertainty as to whether it is a this world or other world experience, and refers to the quality of the experience of the Wildwood, its naturalness and the size of the trees, oak with hazel, ash and beech, the leaf cover blocking out the sky, with the whole wood radiating an immense power. Mériém Clay-Egerton has given a vivid description of just such an experience:

> "Many years ago, when I was what I now consider a very impressionable child, I was introduced to (or it was introduced to me: it matters little now) a very large, tall larch tree. It was, in fact, the only tree in a small copse of mixed trees. How it came to be where it was was not mine to question but simply to enjoy. For me it was a gateway to other places and other times.
>
> The one thing that still strikes me is the overpowering sensation of utter stillness and quietness which this old larch radiated over the whole area of the copse. It seemed to be held in place by what appeared, at least to

me, as a thick impenetrable undergrowth boundary. If one was, however, given leave or licence to enter the area then this insurmountable barrier parted to allow you through, much in the same way as a knife cuts through butter. In those days, because I lived close by, I used to come and go at will. This tree was, I found, so pure and calming that to me it became a sacred spot in a place of unlimited beauty.

Its trunk was old, with deep ridged channels and prominent ribs in its bark. These were homes for many varieties of moss and lichens and their associated lifeforms. Whether they performed any actual service for the tree was not a question which I ever asked or expected an answer to. This tree gave me an aura of beauty and yet utter solemnity while at the same time providing me with a backrest as I sat peacefully among its gnarled and twisted roots.

I used to sit there with closed eyes, hearing and feeling the silence until slowly the tree began to talk to me in faint whispers, which slowly rose to a crescendo as its needles shivered and shook in the open air. Sitting as I was amongst its roots, any wind was invisible to me, but the tree's crown could be tossing and swaying as it caught the particles of sunlight, moonlight and starlight and transmitted them to illuminate the glade below with shimmering radiances - golden during the daytime, but a mind-boggling transformation of silvery-greyish-blueness at night-time.

The pathways which led one imperceptibly away from the foot of the larch tree led one far away into a world of towering trunks with interlacing branches forming a roof, somewhere above my head. Wherever my feet trod on these pathways I left no trace whatsoever upon the ground. I was just a wraith which flitted between these tall living columns of an immense barely-lit natural temple, which welcomed me with a muted hush - a vibrational silence is the only way I can describe it.

Sometimes locations offered by these pathways were totally unexpected. I once encountered what appeared to be a blighted, twisted, scrubby woodland with nothing to recommend it in any way. However, once I had looked beyond this illusion I realised that I could see the individual tree spirits which showed me none of these gnarled twistings. I learnt from them that these woods were not actually blighted, but mainly bowed with old age. However, the land had over many long years grown poor due to leaching-out of trace elements by the acidic waters which fed these trees. They grew very slowly and became these twisted, gnarled specimens, bent to better stand against the prevailing winds. That in those days I found it possible to walk the pathways of illusion in this world and go beyond them into the secret pathways in total freedom and so encounter these trees when they were still young and vibrant remains now only in my memory.

Some paths led me towards forests which had never appeared to have had a youthful spell even in disoriented differential time. The trunks of these trees grew tall and thick: some, indeed, needed several people to interlink arms and hands in order to span them. These trees left me with a deep sense of awe, especially when I thought of their strength, age and solidity. Due to age, these trees often appeared to split around ground-level and if a man or a woman stood within this split they could by empathetic vibrations become at one with its life-force. Despite the hollowness of these trunks, these trees were not dead, as was clearly demonstrated by their huge leafy crowns which appear to sweep through the very heavens themselves.

I knew then that all I needed lay behind the living, shimmering green curtain of the boundary undergrowth. This was all that was needed to divide me from the normal loop of time in which I ought to live from that other one, which permitted me to walk quite happily in the woodlands and along tree-lined pathways which lay deep in the fields of infinite disoriented time itself. Long may they continue to live and exist within the land of memory."[13]

What is happening when we walk through the woods? The trees themselves cut us off from the outside world: they make us look at close quarters, both at the wood itself and at ourselves. All three of the writers quoted so far in this chapter have mentioned the frequent sense of disorientation, even on the part of those who generally have a very good sense of direction.

The wood is alive, and thus it changes, not just with the seasons but over a longer timespan as well. It is deceptive in that, for example, you think it is going to be ever so easy to find a particular tree again, perhaps one that you have chosen for a special purpose. But then, when you go back some time later, things are subtly different: the trees seem to have moved and you can be left confused and uncertain unless you accept this as part of the nature of the woods, their own way of protecting their secrets.

Our senses can become attuned and, as a consequence, we can be changed, usually in a very positive way. We use all our senses, including the subtler ones, hearing the different sounds and echoes in different parts of the wood and become aware of the variety of scents which can be detected, merging to create an aromatic environment which causes adjustments to our subtle being.

Clearly there are several interlocking reasons why woods are so popular with pagans.

Firstly, they are wild - some are primaeval forests which have never known the plough. On entering such a wood we come into the very presence of the God and the Goddess.

Even if we cannot see them, woods are a haven for the nature spirits, and part of us can certainly sense and interact with them.

There is a high measure of concealment in a wood - we can hide (or even get lost) more easily than outside. It is a place of secrets and rituals can be performed with less chance of interference.

The light is different because it is filtered through the leaves and branches and, just like the light from the Full Moon, everything it shines upon changes to a more magical state.

The Wild Wood is like another state of being, in the same way that the dream state is: it can change our consciousness, as Robin Ellis points out. He advocates spending time in these haunted forests, with long periods of meditation. saying:

> *"...it is a journey as much into your own soul as it is into the silent reaches of the forest, and none have made the Otherworld journey into the Wildwood and have returned unchanged by the experience!".*[26]

Just as entering a wood cuts us off from the outside world and its concerns, so, when we leave a wood, there is a very definite feeling of returning to everyday reality. It is like having visited another country.

Above all, the trees themselves are alive - they have a wisdom which only becomes apparent as we get to know them, and the energy and wisdom of a whole forest of trees is far greater even than their sum would suggest. So we enter into the presence of great wisdom when we enter a wood.

Not too far from where I live is an area of ancient woodland - generally recognised to be a survival of primaeval forest that has never seen the plough. Immediately on entering the wood, even during the daytime, there is a tremendous power which can be sensed by many. It has a very definite boundary but, once within, one is freed from the present-day and can wander in both space and time. Large spreading oaks in open grassland are the most striking feature - one half expects Robin Hood to come riding by! But adjoining this is a thicker, denser wood with large old holly trees, great beeches, hawthorns, ash, birch and many more besides - it is truly a sacred grove. Several rituals have taken place here that I know of, and it has clearly been a secret sacred place of the Old Religion for hundreds of years. I certainly feel the presence of those who have gone before me.

Denise Hiley describes a path through an ancient wood which she calls Aphrodite's Way:

"A thin haphazard row of Oak and Hazel trees on either side of the Way cast a swaying dappled leaf shadows on the blessed earth and upon you. In the breeze is a scent of fresh life filled with blossom, grass and earth. In this place you feel the sensuous desire to lay in the grass under the trees and breathe in the freshness of the air through every pore. Wantonly you give in. There is an Oak tree here almost like a seat (the throne of Zeus) which one can climb up and sit in to survey the kingdom of growth and yearning to bear forth life. ... Entering the opposite side of the path one finds oneself

in low growing Scots Pine; Oak; Larch; Beech and Birch trees. No vegetation, except fungi. grows here. There is a tense, watchful quietness, as if the very spirit of the wood is hushed into silence, probing our very heart and mind in a way which is nature's power alone."[40]

Sacred Groves

The whole of the wild wood is the special place of the Goddess and the God. But within the wood certain locations have something extra - difficult to define precisely, but a 'sense of place' which says, quite distinctly, "here I am". They may be clearings, often where the trees surrounding it form a circle - a sacred ring of trees. There is power here - the interaction between the trees somehow providing a focus that can be sensed.

Sacred groves are frequently referred to in connection with the Druids, but in practice little is definitely known. Trees and tree clumps are alive and the implication of this is that they can also die. Obviously this is true of individual trees, but clumps, too, even with natural regeneration, will probably die naturally over time. The only way the Druids' sacred groves (and, from further back, Alfred Watkins' mark clumps) could possibly have survived is by some form of tending or care by individuals or communities to whom they were important or special.

Much of this must also be speculation, but it might be possible to recognise a sacred grove by its surviving characteristics. Tony Wedd does this in referring to a clump in Wiltshire :

> "The clump is mostly of beech, but also carries Ash, Elm, Elder, Yew, Box, Hornbeam, Holly, Ivy, Sycamore,

An Ancient Beech Grove on the Isle of Man

Privet, May and Willow. I Fancy it is an old Celtic Grove, planted with the 13 trees of the tree calendar, which were also the names of the Beth-Luis-Nion alphabet letters"[88]

To illustrate the feelings which people have had on entering a sacred grove, I give some examples, two of which happen to be from the county of Sussex and both of which were severely damaged by the hurricane of 1987. One is a clump of pines and one is of beech.

The pine clump will ever be associated in my mind with its role as a marker on Alfred Watkins' leys. There is something uplifting about even a solitary Scots Pine. When I walk into a clump of them I feel I am walking into a different world. It is so pure and fresh it is as if all my worries and depression fall away. New hope springs up and even joy. I once wrote some lines when in a pine clump in Dorset, part of which went:

"The Scots Pine's function is to surround, protect and balance a whole area ... The energy is quiet and sustains. It stills the mind. In the wind, in the clumps on the hilltops, then also does the Scots Pine uplift. It opens the doors of perception to the possibilities. It uplifts the spirit to experience and action."

The clump of Scots Pine known as Gill's Lap on one of the highest points on Ashdown Forest in Sussex is perhaps for me the archetypal tree clump, though I haven't seen it for several years, and Jimmy Goddard tells me that the hurricane of 1987 did much damage. Certainly, in my memory, it could be seen from many miles away on the Greensand Ridge above Crockham Hill, in Kent. Tony Wedd, who lived nearby at Chiddingstone, introduced it to me, and I

An Ancient Hilltop Beech Grove, still used for rituals

will always associate it with his ideas about the alignment of clumps on the Kent/Sussex border, of which it was a focal point. Rather than describe it myself, I shall leave it to A.A. Milne, author of "*The House at Pooh Corner*", who calls it Galleon's Lap :

> "*They walked on, thinking of This and That, and by-and-by they came to an enchanted place on the very top of the Forest called Galleons Lap, which is sixty-something trees in a circle; and Christopher Robin knew that it was enchanted because nobody had ever been able to count whether it was sixty-three or sixty-four, not even when he tied a piece of string round each tree after he had counted it. Being enchanted, its floor was not like the floor of the Forest, gorse and bracken and heather, but close-set grass, quiet and smooth and green. It was the only place in the Forest where you could sit down carelessly, without getting up again almost at once and looking for somewhere else. Sitting there they could see the whole world spread out until it reached the sky, and whatever there was all the world over was with them in Galleons Lap.*"[55]

It is a very special place.

Also in Sussex, on the top of the South Downs, is a beech clump planted some 200 years ago within the prehistoric bank and ditch of Chanctonbury Ring. I suspect that this is the place Doreen Valiente is referring to when she writes:

> "*... [it] has a curious history. It does not seem to like outsiders. People who have gone there, moved by idle curiosity, having heard some rumour of its connection with the Old Religion, have had strange and*

frightening experiences when they tried to perform some mocked-up rite for a laugh. Personally, however, I have always felt a sense of welcome there - so long as one did not take liberties."[84]

Doreen Valiente also makes reference to a former local custom of going up to the Ring to see the sun rise on May Day morning and to the legend that if you ran round it seven times at midnight the Devil would appear. Putting these together, she suggests that they are evidence that the place was traditionally used for pagan rituals at the festivals.[82]

R. Thurston Hopkins also refers to the significance of the place:

"I am not a Sussex man myself, but in spite of the fact I can never see Chanctonbury Ring without feeling a thrill in my blood. It has an enchantment - a sort of elemental sweetness - which is not easily explained. The Ring is not merely a topographical fact to me - it is ten thousand Sussex men who sleep in Flanders, part of the race-consciousness. The spell of Chanctonbury is the very innermost significance, the truest wealth of England. For a thousand years the soil of it has been mixed with human thought and substance. It is the heritage of the sons and daughters of Sussex, and with its magic has won our hearts to a passionate devotion."[41]

The trees were severely affected by the 1987 storm and, I gather, by a subsequent fire. Poet and artist Jill Smith evokes the spirit of the place, in her poem entitled *"Chanctonbury Rings"*:

Once eagles wheeled and soared above.....
I touched you,
lived in a small hollow,
walked your high spine at dawn,
slept under your whispering trees
on dark, dark nights
and dreamed your memories;
walked magic on your dark, soft earth
under those tall, dark trees:
faeries and elementals murmured round me then.
Dark in the night,
magic in the day
under your tall, dark dome.

Returning,
I climb a sheer and unfamiliar hill,
walk an unaccustomed path
and you are not what I expected.
Now your rings stand bare,
as they did at their beginnings -
fleshly circles on your
serpent head.

I had forgotten
the wind came
and wrenched your trees out
taking your dark mystery,
leaving your primal naked reality
windswept and wind-torn.

I feel the energy of that night,
would have stood with you
wild on the heaving earth
as the great trees
fell around me -
ecstatic, not caring
if I lived or died.

Now all is quiet.
Stumps stand
like remnants of an ancient graveyard,
but young trees
spring straight and strong.

Around your circle
some still stand,
spiral trunks
entwined in spiral helical embrace
echoing the serpent patterns
of the earth.

Some lifetime
I shall come again
and maybe then
the dark canopy will rise above
and eagles soar and wheel once more.....

Jill Smith 1990

I have known other beech clumps. They all induce in me that strange mixture and excitement that opens up possibilities and raises the spirit. I would always go to a beech grove if I felt depressed - the beech is strangely comforting. My friend, Kay Watkins, wrote to me of her feelings for beech:

"I know that beech trees have been special to me for many years. I find beech breath-takingly beautiful to look at, the colour and texture of the leaves and the delicate buds always get me excited. About five years ago I was visiting a friend in Lancashire. It was a town that I was totally unfamiliar with so I asked her to recommend an interesting walk to get a feel of the place. I walked up a hilly lane and enjoyed the complete contrast to the flatness I was used to - just seeing the

A remote and magical spot on the Isle of Man - a beech tree on a bank near a stream is a powerful place for meditation or individual ritual

shapes of places from a height is a treat. It was quite a cold, damp day in February. I was in a typical February state, bleak and dull. When I recognised a small beech tree I wasn't surprised: it might have been growing there for me at that time. I was weary and needed comfort as I lay against the trunk and half-dozed for perhaps twenty minutes. The tree gave me exactly what I needed. It was all so natural and simple. I felt held physically and comforted spiritually."

I once wrote the following lines while sitting in a beech grove:

"Beech is closely linked with the Earth - it covers large areas and helps to link the human spirit firmly in the physical plane. It is grounded in action on the physical plane - in long, steady, worthwhile action, and helps to promote an inner knowing. It also sustains at a fundamental level."

I know instinctively that they are used throughout the country by pagans for their rites, and have found evidence on more than one occasion that they have been so used. In many ways they are ideal - the lofty smooth-barked trees and the clear ground underneath seem ideal for gatherings, perhaps large gatherings on occasion. Autumn always seems the right time to gather. They have a totally different feel to the pines.

Dingley Dell is a sacred grove in a very different location to those I have already mentioned. It is located on the edge of a large northern city, in that intermediate zone where the miles of solid built-up housing give way to fields, on a rise that enables one to look out over the whole city. The area once consisted of large detached houses in their own grounds. One of the grandest was demolished a few years ago -

perhaps in expectation of the planning permission for housing development that was never forthcoming.

The grounds were large and had been extensively planted with trees at least 200 years ago. They have been neglected for many years. There had also been an orchard and an extensive belt of planting along the north side of the site.

A friend was led there by "chance" a few years ago and was amazed by the feel of the place. She started to go there to meditate and still uses it regularly. I was taken there for the first time at dusk and followed the path round as the sun was setting and the sky gradually turned dark. This seems to be the right time of day to go there as the "normal" magical atmosphere is greatly intensified.

One enters the land through a small gap next to the footpath and immediately there is a feeling of wildness - suburbia is left far behind. Ahead is a tall beech tree. One instinctively senses that this is the guardian of the site and it is natural to stop here for a few minutes before going on. The tree likes to be embraced and it takes three of us, holding hands, to make a ring around its trunk. There are holly trees here as well, with girths thicker than I have ever seen. Holly grows very slowly and I have begun to suspect that this may truly be a sacred grove dating back much further than we had ever thought.

Moving on, one goes through an avenue of yews. It is natural to walk slowly, taking up a natural rhythmic gait, as if in walking meditation. Entering the yew avenue is to enter into the dark - that passageway through to the Otherworld. Everyone instinctively falls silent. To one side is a large old yew tree, its branches low down on the ground. One realises that here is somewhere very special and protected. It is possible to feel the aura surrounding this tree/place physically and there is a definite barrier which will admit or not as it wills. Within the confines of the tree one feels both protected and with a heightened sensitivity to one's surroundings. One begins to be aware of the interest of nature spirits.

Reluctantly moving on, we reach the far side of the wood, close to a modern motor road. The traffic noise does not intrude, however, as we turn to start the walk back. Here is one of the wonders of this place - a great belt of mature trees. Hornbeams, taller and straighter than I have ever seen before, together with beech. The path winds its way between these huge trunks, coming up to meet each one in turn, and then changing direction as it passes - a succession of small clearings and thickets alternate. The light of the setting sun reflects off the bark of these large beings - one can sense the Earth Spirit in this place, and one falls silent in awe and joy. The regular rhythm of the path and the trees induces a state of mind quite different from the everyday and it is in a totally different frame of mind that one finds oneself back at the sentinel beech.

It is a very special place and I am privileged to have been taken there.

Forgotten Land - the Boundary between the Worlds

The corners of fields, hedges and marginal land seem to be mentioned surprisingly often as witch meeting places or associated with them.

Margaret Murray quotes several examples of witches gathering on heaths and commons in "The Witch Cult in Western Europe".[59]

Field corners are awkward places. They provide shelter, with the meeting point between hedges and, particularly if the land slopes down into the corner, can be very secluded.

Sometimes the neglected land may result in a tree clump or, because of the drainage pattern, a pond may form or a dew pond be constructed with access from more than one field.

Doreen Valiente received what she felt were psychic communications about a coven of witches who lived in Surrey in the early 19th Century. They held outdoor meetings in the corner of one of the fields owned by their leader[85].

I have some quite vivid memories of what I take to be a previous lifetime somewhere in England at some time in the past, to put it no more precisely. We have finished haymaking and are celebrating with food and drink and circle dancing in the corner of a field which is surrounded on three sides by a wood. The feeling which comes through is not just of celebration but a sense of power and rightness, which I have also felt in this lifetime in certain witchcraft rituals.

Apart from this, I have found the edge between a field and a wood to be immensely powerful, perhaps because of the contrast between the enclosed and hidden and the wide open spaces - the ability to see without being seen. The edge of a wood is a powerful place for a ritual as one is concealed but can see the sky. The act of moving out into the field and then back 'home' to the circle in the wood is a very powerful symbolic act.

Nigel Aldcroft Jackson draws attention to the fact that the witch was called the 'Hedge Sitter' or 'Hedge Rider' (Haegtessa in Middle English). The hedge was seen as the boundary between this world and the Otherworld, which the witch could cross.[42]

Although today many hedges have been removed, many still remain and are a haven for wildlife. Many are very old, as the hedge dating technique developed by Hooper based on the number of tree species within a specified distance makes clear.

The theme which links these varying sites is that they are "between" - a state which in the Celtic view has a certain quality and power. Field corners and hedges, and the commons which were often on a parish boundary, or in "No Man's Land", had this quality of "betweenness" and therefore power. It is the same principle as that whereby the magic circle is recognised as being "between the worlds". Jeremy Harte, on examining the folklore of Dorset, and particularly place-related accounts of ghost sightings, has drawn attention to their appearance on parish boundaries in unusual numbers. This seems to emphasise the power of the place which is neither one nor the other.[38]

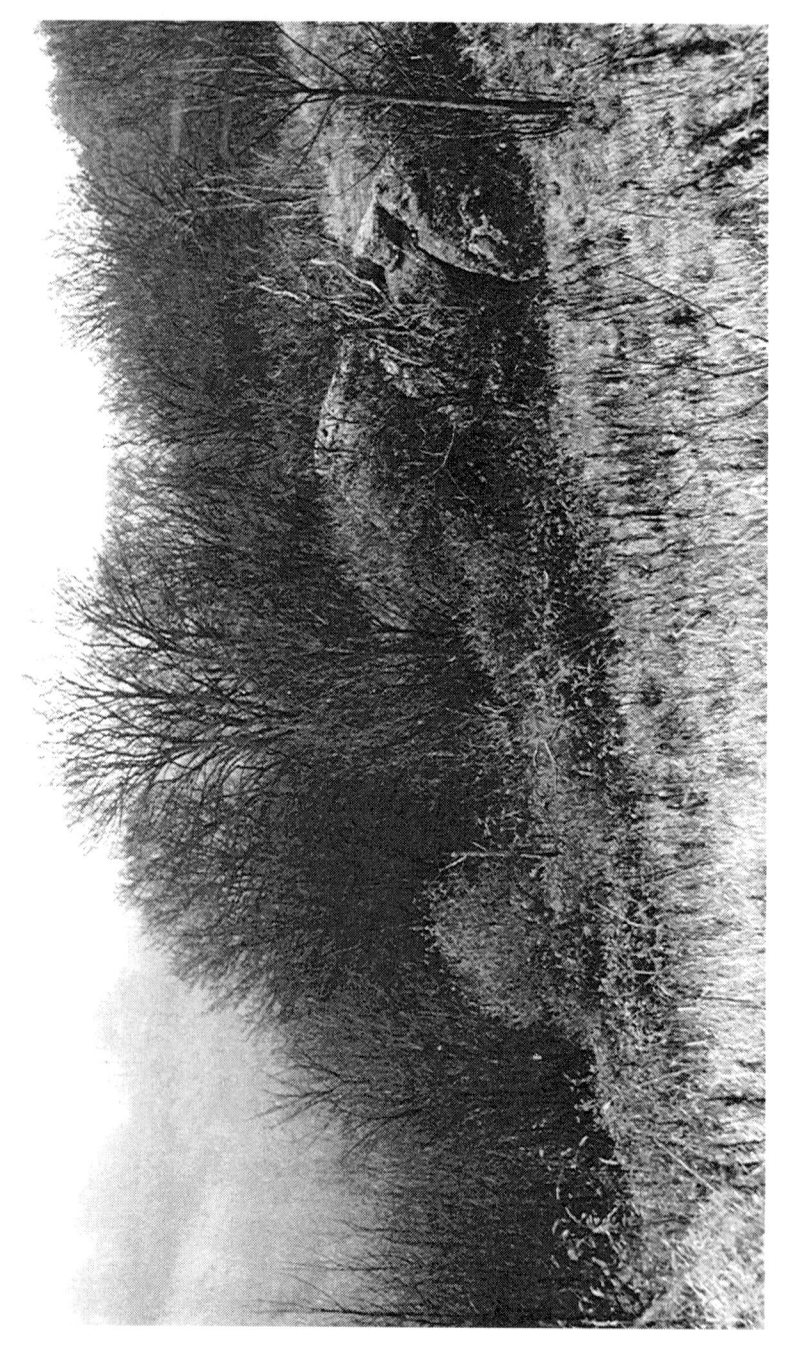

A rock outcrop known to have been used for ritual since pre-Christian times

CHAPTER 4

THE BODY OF THE EARTH GODDESS

We live in and on the Earth; the fertile soil nourishes us and beneath everything is the bedrock, the Earth from which we all emerge.

The underlying rock determines in large measure the character of the land. The distinctive nature of the rolling Sussex Downs, the rugged Cornish coast and the harsh Pennine uplands is largely a result of the quality of the rock which forms them.

Just as we may accept the existence of the human aura and the living spirit of trees and other plants, so rock has its hidden dimension - its other reality. Michael Bentine asked a medium why some parts of the countryside gave him a great feeling of security and peace whereas others made him feel uncomfortable and nervous. The answer was that, over the generations, people have imprinted their personalities onto the chalk and that Bentine, as a sensitive, was picking this up.[3] This echoes Dion Fortune's comment in *"The Goat-Foot God"* that the best place to get experiences of a psychic or intuitive nature was on the chalk.[28]

Little Almscliff Crag

We come from the Earth and we return to the Earth. The cave has clearly been important from ancient times for both shelter and ritual purposes and the old cave paintings indicate that they were perceived as being very special places. The cave, the gap between rocks, and even the hollow in the earth are all places we can go to be close to the Earth Goddess. They have a practical function, in sheltering fire from wind and prying eyes, but by their nature (and their rarity) they remain very special.

They are often hidden, as Arthur Ransome recounts:

> *"Roger heard her, in spite of the noise of the waterfall. He did not hear the words, but there was something urgent in her voice that was enough to put the trout out of his head. What had she found? He came, running, and found her looking under the clump of heather into a dark hole in the wall of grey rock. It was a hole, narrower at the top than at the bottom, big enough to let a stooping man use it as a doorway, and yet so well sheltered by the rock which, just here, leaned outward over it, and so deep in the shadow of the thick bushy heather that was growing out of cracks in the stone above it and on either side of it, that it would have been easy to think it was no more than a cleft in the rock, and easier still not to notice it at all. The two explorers crouched together, and tried to see into the black darkness inside."*[66]

Caves are certainly still being used for ritual purposes. Robert Cochrane has written a moving account of a ritual which took place in a cave high up on a hillside, where a fire was lit and invocations were successfully employed[14]; and Dion Fortune, in her novel *"The Sea Priestess"*, has Morgan le Fay and Wilfrid Maxwell performing rituals in a cave high up on the sea cliffs.[29]

Another likely pagan ritual site is Lud's Cave or Lud's Church, of which Stephanie Wilson paints a graphic picture:

> "Lud's church is perhaps one of the oldest and most unusual churches in England. Formed from a huge natural fissure in the hillside its great lichen filmed walls of rock are striking. With the open sky as its roof and concealed by trees it is hardly surprising to find it rooted so deeply in romance and legend. ... Naturally camouflaged by trees the church was virtually inaccessible to those who did not know of its whereabouts. ... It is hard not to be affected by the ancient atmosphere of the place as you descend the worn stone steps leading over eighty feet down into the rocky chasm. The lichen, long ferns and trees growing out of the rocks are set deeply in the past ... one wonders also if Lud's cave wasn't originally a place for pagan worship; since 'lud' is the name given to a sacred grove where sacrifice was performed. ... When I visited Lud's cave for the first time I was struck by the feminine aura of the place. The rock was gentle, welcoming."[92]

Denise Hiley writes about an outcrop of rocks known as the Devil's Cave, which enables one to see without being seen:

> "In recent times the cave has fallen in several places but one can easily squeeze between the rocks to enter. Through the gap one encounters steps, worn and crumbling, leading southward to a 'window' ledge in the rock where one can sit, unobserved from without, overlooking a beautiful panorama stretching for miles."[40]

In those landscapes where caves are absent, the hollow in the land takes on added importance. This might, of course, be a whole secret valley, such as that described by Arthur Ransome:

> *"They hurried on until they stood below the waterfall. Above them the water poured down noisily from ledge to ledge of rock, and they could go no farther without climbing up the rocks beside the falling water or getting out of the long winding gully that the stream had carved for itself in the moor. ... Neither of them had expected anything like what they found when they scrambled over the top. It was a little valley in the moorland, shut in by another waterfall at the head of it, not a hundred yards away, and by slopes of rock and heather that rose so steeply that when the explorers looked up they could see nothing but the sky above them. In there it was as if the blue mountains did not exist. The valley might have been hung in air, for all that they could see outside it, except when they turned round and looked back, from the top of the waterfall they had climbed, to the moorland, the woods and the hills on the other side of the lake.*
>
> *'It's a lovely place for brigands,' said the boy.*
>
> *'It's just the place for Peter Duck,' said the able-seaman. 'It's the most secret valley that ever there was in the world.'"*[66]

On the chalk wolds and downs you get pits that have been dug at some time in the past, perhaps hundreds of years ago. Along with Ian Taylor[79] I suspect that chalk pits could have been used for ritual purposes as well as having more utilitarian functions. They are practical in that they are

The Chiding Stone - an ancient ritual meeting place in Kent

sheltered both from the wind and from prying eyes, as well as being close to the Earth. Nicholson[60] refers to the popular belief that chalk pits were haunted and Ethel Rudkin[71] tells of a legend related to Queen Maud's Hole near Scunthorpe, that Queen Maude was successfully hidden there and that at midnight her spirit is to be seen walking.

Taylor has also drawn our attention to the significance of "Old Wife" place names. There are several Old Wife Pits in the East Riding and one might well suppose that these could be sites where adherents of the old religion met and carried out their rites in worship of the Goddess. They certainly have a very powerful feeling at times, as he relates:

> "Anyone ... who is sufficiently inwardly tranquil and open to the influence of the landscape, cannot fail to be struck by the uncanny quality which the chalk 'breathes out' ... When the weather has entered a relatively rain free period, but when cloud cover is moderately dense and uniform, but not too low - when the prevailing light is evenly spread over the landscape, with no parts over bright or too deep in shadow - when the wind is still or gently fitful, a magic prevails everywhere upon the Wolds, and it comes from within the chalk. ... It is the essential inner spirit of the earth here - immemorial and profoundly mystical - and nowhere is it so potent as upon the edges of these curious chalk pits. Every time I visit a relatively unspoilt pit I step into this magic. ... deep unconscious imagery can arise in these places, and a mood of chastening solemnity will prevail."[79]

Doreen Valiente mentions several occasions when hollows on the Downs were used for rituals. Being sheltered from the wind and from distant views, a small fire became more practicable:

"The scent of the incense mingled with the woodsmoke from the fire and the odours of the fallen leaves and the earth we danced upon. Above, the stars shone intermittently through the clouds, and the wind blew gently, with the chill of approaching winter. We were in a hollow, to screen the fire from any watchful eyes; so we could not see any lights of the surrounding countryside. The modern world seemed to have faded away and left us in a sort of timelessness."[85]

Places where the rock comes to the surface were from earliest times considered in some way special - places of power.

Up on the Yorkshire Wolds, not far from where I live, is a mass of concrete-like breccia, left behind as the ice retreated at the end of the last Ice Age. It is sited near the very top of a dry valley cut into the chalk, with views out over the Humber into Lincolnshire. The stone is over 10 feet high and several times as long.

There is a persistent local legend that St. Augustine erected a cross on top and preached from the stone on his mission to England. It is said that he did this because he found the stone venerated by the local people. He is also supposed to have led his converts down the valley and baptised them in a spring. Even into the present century, Christian services have been held at the stone. Until the 18th Century there were many old oak trees around the site and, in the early 19th Century, it is described as being in an open space within a wood.

The place has a strange atmosphere. It is on private land, but is close to a public footpath and can be seen clearly, although hidden completely from the nearby public road. It has a serious air about it, even sombre. A friend I took there described it as having a very strong 'male' energy.

Clearly this stone was recognised as a special place since before the time of Augustine and has undoubtedly been a centre for both the Old Religion and Christianity for hundreds of years.

Another site with a strong atmosphere is The Devil's Pulpit. It is an outcrop of rock on the side of a valley half a mile from the nearest settlement. The pulpit itself is a freestanding mass of rock - a twelve-foot high pillar of sandstone in full view of the road running up the far side of the valley, but hidden by a spur of land from the village itself. There is evidence that until recent times there was a clump of Scots Pines on that spur, but only two now remain. Nevertheless, they contribute powerfully to the 'feel' of the place, and sensitives have felt that there had been joyous dancing there at one time. There seem to be some carvings on the rock, suggesting a connection with the Moon Goddess, and there is a local legend that it was a witches' meeting place until perhaps as late as the 19th Century.

Bob Dickinson visited the site at midnight under a November Full Moon. He seemed to lose all awareness of time and space, saying "It was as if I was entering another realm altogether ...". He wrote the following lines on his experience:

He parks his car
And leaving the present behind him
stumbles across the ditch
through the parting in the hedge
and dragging his now aging body across the winter field.
in slow sinking treads of the rain-sodden clay
He reaches the wire.

He feels its sharpness cut an eye in his soft flesh
and for a moment watches his life-blood weep in a dying fall
returning to a dark warm mother of his beginning

That rock,
That time,
That hearth-stone of his soul
He merges with the night
"Be still" - there is a whisper in his ear
and entering that ancient sacred space
Listens once more to the heartbeat of his wildness.

Rock and Stone, on the surface immovable and unchangeable, are in fact full of life. Janian Richardson gives a vivid account of approaching the Southstone, near Stanford Bridge, Worcestershire:

> *"I shall never forget the first glimpse I had of the huge grey rock shouldering itself out of the wood, arousing in me all the paternalistic fears stored up since childhood. It had been a long climb to reach the place, up a path oozing with red mud, beneath bare trees. The time of year was mid-November and the woodlands were swallowed in desolation. ... We came to a spot where a single birch tree stood high above the briars and bracken. A narrow track wound from its roots into the woods. We could hear the gurgling of a stream. Carefully, picking my way with the hazel stick we had cut the day before, I followed Ray through the dismal trees. Then I saw it, grim and forbidding, towering ahead. We emerged from the wood and stood in front of the rock. It was like a grey fortress, crowned by the forest and encircled by twisted elder trees, with a dark cave hewn out of its base."*[69]

Before the days of quarrying and railway cuttings, rock outcrops were, particularly in some parts of the country, very rare and therefore took on a magical aura. This seems to come from the very Earth itself and might well be seen by those who were sensitive to such things in terms of a 'presence' or, more specifically, as nature spirits and fairies. Paul Devereux has called some of them "the mind-gates of Gaia": places where we can interact with the Earth Spirit.[21] Certainly the evidence of the examples given above would indicate that they were recognised in former times as being sacred and became special places where rituals were performed.

St. Helen's Well - a sacred place where the waters of the Goddess still flow.

CHAPTER 5

THE WATERS OF LIFE

Water is vital to our survival - certainly physically, but also on the deeper spiritual levels. We need only look at the popularity of trips to the seaside, lakes and rivers to see that water holds some deep attraction. Perhaps it is because our body is mostly made up of water; perhaps because water represents the emotions and feelings that are so often cut off from full expression in our modern way of life.

Water is, of course, present in the landscape in a variety of forms, and features frequently in descriptions of sites. Constantly in motion, through springs, streams and rivers and flowing out to the ocean, water is drawn by the power of the sun only to fall as rain onto the hills and mountains, soaking back into the Earth. Known scientifically as the hydrological cycle, this transformation can teach us a lot about the nature of cycles and our own potential for living in accordance with them.

Sacred Springs

These are truly magical places, where the water flows from the very womb of the Earth Goddess. Despite lowering of the water table in recent years, many of these springs still survive, issuing pure water in a flow which has continued uninterrupted since ancient times. Many of these springs are called "Holy Wells", and it is clear in many cases that they were holy a long time before the advent of Christianity.

The sound and sight of the water can help induce in us a meditative state, where we are stilled and drift into a communion with the Goddess. Edna Whelan and Ian Taylor conjure up this atmosphere vividly:

> *"...there are places where peace and tranquillity have existed for thousands of years. To visit these places and linger in their atmosphere is a nourishing and revivifying experience. It seems that we step into a world where time is suspended and where the mysterious life-spirit is remarkably concentrated. There are many sites which have this special quality - none more so than the ancient Holy Wells and Sacred Springs, long acknowledged as places of great sanctity ... Imagine a junction of ancient footpaths on a hillside beyond a village, or a leafy hollow in a wood, or perhaps the corner of a meadow with a group of hawthorns or a craggy outcrop on a moor, places where the numinous qualities of the planet still persist. Introduce the sound of gently flowing water and one has the sites of the typical Holy Well."*[90]

Until well into the present century springs were important in that they provided the only pure water for a village. Many others acquired a reputation for healing or prophetic qualities, and the numinous quality in the immediate environment of the spring has long been experienced in terms of water spirits, the "undines" of Greek legend. From ancient times, springs were sacred to the Earth Spirit, places where people could go to be healed, both physically and in spirit, as well as opening up the prophetic sense.

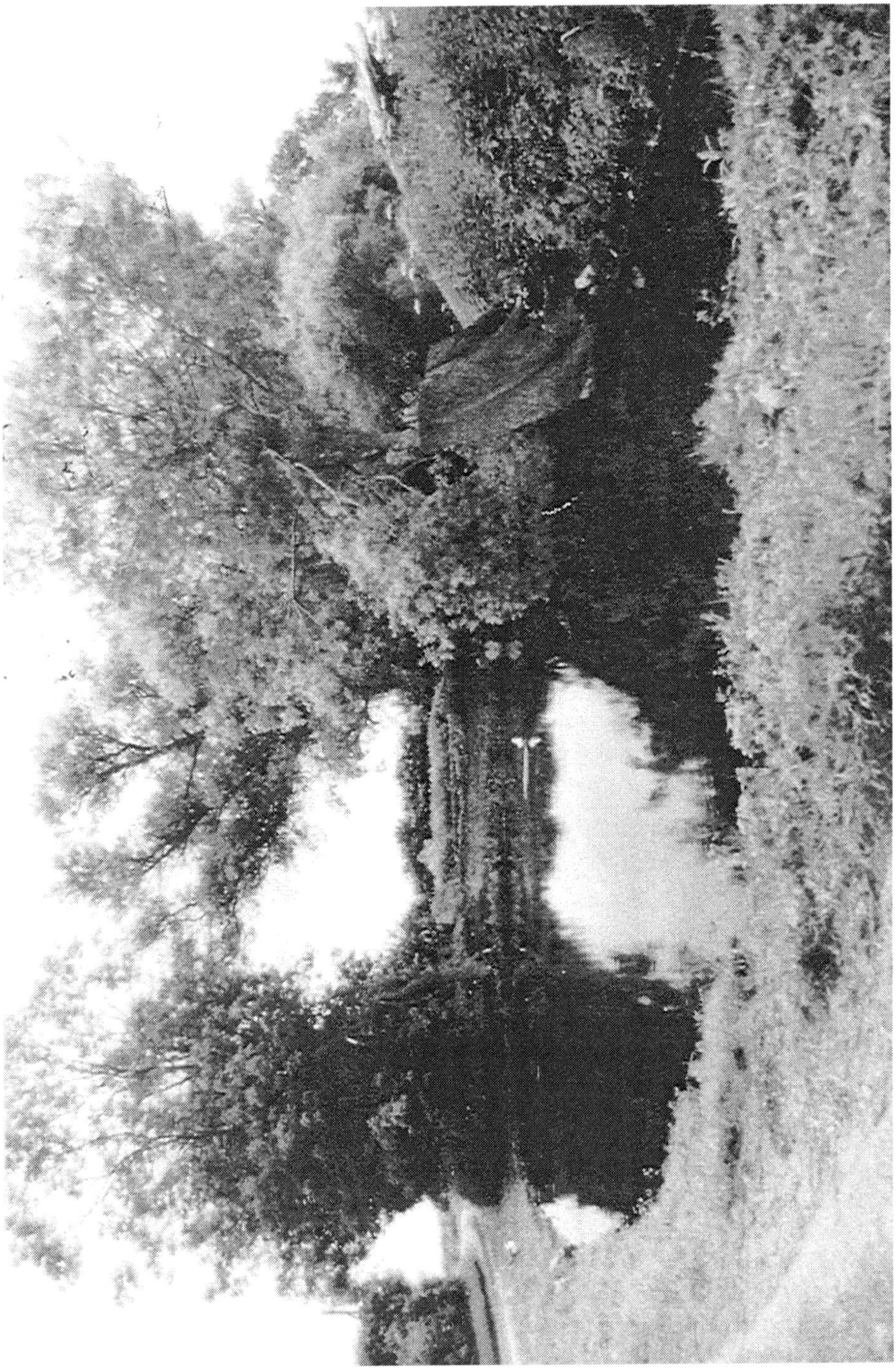

For a long time, springs remained in a natural state, though certain very special and magical trees, particularly hawthorn and elder, are to be found growing directly above the spring, embodying the essence of the Goddess. Offerings began to be left and many springs are still known as Rag Wells, where a strip of rag is tied onto the tree as an offering or for a wish to be granted.

There is something very powerful about seeing, hearing and feeling the pure clear water coming up from within the Earth. The feelings evoked are really beyond words, but I will try to give some idea of the feel of the place with descriptions of two examples of springs local to where I live.

St Helen's Well is near a minor road which runs along the side of a valley only a mile or so outside a small market town. A footpath leaves the road and follows a series of steps down perhaps 30 yards to an open patch of ground surrounded by trees, mostly ash, thorn and elder. The first indication of the well is a still pool of water held in place by a trapezoid of concrete. The water is so clear that you have to look twice to see it at all. It emanates from a small cave at the narrow end of the pool. The cave is in the steep hillside and immediately above is a large old elder - clearly the guardian of the site - the Elder Mother. In its branches is a notice informing the reader that the local Girl Guides cleared out the spring and tidied up the area a few years previously. The cave goes back deep into the Earth - from it flows a clear stream of pure water beside which it is possible to crouch in a meditational state, protected from the vagaries of the world, for this special period.

Someone else still comes here - there is an offering of coloured wool tied to one of the tree branches directly above the flowing spring. Laboriously, with knees bent, I fill my plastic bottle with water using the only ladle I have - the small plastic top of the bottle itself. My limbs ache as the rhythm of dipping the cap into the flowing stream and pouring it into the bottle becomes hypnotic. But at last the bottle is full and, with weary legs, I straighten up, give thanks to the Goddess of the place and make my way back up to the road.

Lud's Well is hidden and secret. Coming along the green track on the top of the Wolds it looks like another small wood nestling in the corner of the field. I am with one who knows the place, however, and instead of walking past to the farm beyond, we part the trees and enter the wood. Ahead, there is a steep slope and, after negotiating thorn branches, nettles and mud, we find ourselves on the banks of a gentle stream.

Opposite us is a yew tree, contributing to a pervading air of peace and permanence. Someone has tied rags to its branches in offering. Where does the stream come from? The only way is to wade up to the source. Slowly and carefully we make our way up to where several springs are cascading out of the hillside, some with considerable force.

This spot is clearly special and magical, not least because the springs can be neither heard nor seen nor even suspected from outside the wood. It is a natural amphitheatre - a place where offerings have been left in the past and are still left today. It is a place apart from the everyday world, where magical things can and do happen. Bob Dickinson, with his poetic vision, has written this evocative piece:

> *"A steep scramble down an ivy-covered slope leads one into a place of great natural beauty alive with the earth spirit force. Luxuriant and massive fern ground cover, the visual and aural beauty of the undocumented sacred waters cascading over small waterfalls, contribute to a truly magical atmosphere, a positive retreat from the world above.*

The most sensorily significant of the two springs is the one which emerges from the northern hillside. Reaching back into the womblike darkness of Mother Earth the waters issue forth into a small pool, then over an edge being transformed into a miniature cascade."[23]

Streams and Waterfalls

"But it was not the rock that Ray wanted to show me. He led me away to the right. The stream's laughter was much louder now, and there was a waterfall, cascading over the gloomy stones, almost luminous in the greyness. After the sombreness of the climb uphill and the stern appearance of the rock, it was so joyful that I nearly cried. Ray was ahead of me in the stream. "Look here", he said. He showed me a small hollow or grotto among the rocks, vivid with green moss, streaming with crystal threads of water. He plunged his head into the hollow, and I followed suit. The icy coldness took my breath away; the shock flashed down my spine. It was wonderfully refreshing and strengthening."[69]

This was the way Janian Richardson continued the account quoted in the previous chapter. For most of us, sitting by a stream or waterfall is an experience to remember, where it induces a form of elated and meditative state, where part of us tunes in to universal values and we come away with a better sense of proportion in our lives. Waterfalls are the seat of Lethbridge's undines and there are numerous reports of fairies and 'white ladies' being seen. Alex Langstone gives something of the feel of such a place in writing about the White Lady waterfall in Lydford Gorge, Devon:

"The Gorge is an enchanted place of mystery and magic: it is indeed a haunted glade, where one would expect to see Elves and Sprites flitting between tree and river. Tall, slender birch trees sway each side of the river, and a footpath leads away from the falls in both directions. There is a small bridge that will take us over to the opposite bank if we so wish! But I hear a voice calling from the falls. The watery voice of a lady; the Soul of Nature."[46]

Bob Dickinson responds to this voice in a very direct way:

"Under a full harvest moon. Upper Falls, Aysgarth Force: Climbing down to the waters' edge below the falls, crossing rock pools to a solitary boulder, sitting there and listening, eyes closed. The white noise intensity of the cascading waters filling the air. Cupping hands over ears, humming a single sustained tone - my own resonant pitch - for the length of a breath, repeating over and over. Very gradually and very slowly opening the mouth, singing the same pitch but changing its timbre through a filtering process which reveals the overtones comprising that fundamental pitch. Two sounds heard together: the fundamental and the harmonic. On reaching the "Ah" shape of the mouth, slowly closing - still singing the same tone - to return to the original humming. The process repeated over and over again. Something else happening through all this: as the mouth slowly opens, the complex sound of the falls entering through this 'gate', resonating within the vocal chamber of the head, filtered in much the same way as the sung tone is and at the same time. A composite of natural and humanly-produced sound, a feeling of the whole body merging with the rock and water, a coming together of elemental forces."[24]

Fulwood Spa, Sheffield

The essential nature of the waterfall is that the water is in constant motion, but it is never the same water. The waterfall cannot be captured in a box, because it ceases then to have the quality that makes it a waterfall. There are similar lessons to learn in our own lives.

Ponds - Mirrors of Magic

Water flows - as rain, from the hillside spring or well, along the stream-bed, over waterfalls and through gorges - making its way to the sea, which is constantly in motion with its waves and tides.

The still water, when it occurs, is something special, magical. In a small pool, the water can, in certain circumstances, be absolutely still - a mirror more perfect than any which can be made by human hand.

There are many archetypal stories and legends where the pool represents the entrance into the depths of the Earth and of ourselves - those principles represented astrologically by the planetary energies of the Moon and Pluto. Dozmary Pool, in Cornwall, for example, is associated with Arthurian legend. Arthur's sword Excalibur is thrown into the lake. A hand belonging to the Lady of the Lake, rises out of the water, catches the sword and takes it beneath the surface. And Julia Cartwright tells the story of Silent Pool, in Surrey:

> "Here, in the middle of the Duke of Northumberland's park, is the deep glen, surrounded by wooded heights, known as the Silent Pool. A dark tale, which Martin Tupper has made the subject of his 'Stephen Langton', belongs to this lonely spot. King John, tradition says, loved a fair woodman's daughter who lived here, and surprised her in the act of bathing in the pool. The

frightened girl let loose the branch by which she held, and was drowned in the water; and her brother, a goatherd, who at the sound of her scream had rushed in after her, shared the same fate. And still, the legend goes, at midnight you may see a black-haired maiden clasping her arms round her brother in his cow-hide tunic under the clear rippling surface of the Silent Pool."[10]

The number of pagan motifs in such a story suggests that at some time in the past it was a centre for ritual.

Following the retreat of the ice, many natural pools were formed, but artificial ponds, such as the dewponds of the chalk uplands, were constructed with both utilitarian and magical purposes. On this point, Ian Taylor writes:

"That a number of dew ponds have been maintained in good condition by local people, when the need for them as a source of drinking water for livestock was no longer required, is testimony to the existence of some fragments at least of geomantic awareness that have persisted through untold generations of local families into the present day."[79]

He has detected by dowsing lines of energy, force or spirit at numerous dewponds on the Wolds. They were generally circular formations around the dew pond itself, but seem to be affected by nearby hawthorn and elder trees, gateways and cattle tracks. Expanding on this possibility, he says:

"The orgone stimulation at certain of these sites has to be experienced to be realised - as I can testify from

having recently dowsed one. On that occasion the combination of the highly charged field of etheric energy around the site, the brilliant winter sunlight upon the water (increasing the amount of orgone present) and the recent presence of cattle which had been circling and drinking at the pond were intoxicating. Despite a bitterly cold wind (it was December and the site was very exposed at nearly 600 feet) I felt radiantly warm and relaxed as I dowsed the site."[79]

That ponds are powerful places is enshrined in folklore, such as that quoted by Ethel Rudkin about Morton, near Gainsborough:

"In Morton parish there is what appears to be an old pit, always full of water, and very deep, "bottomless", it is said. ... The people call it the "Gymes" (pronounced with a hard g); there are other gymes in the same area but not as large as this one. At midnight a Lady in White rises from the Gymes at Morton, and passes over the surrounding country"[71]

The White Lady sounds very much like a reference to the Moon reflected in the water. There is a strong link between the Moon and water. Astrologically it is the ruler of the sign Cancer, a water sign, and is strongly related to many qualities, such as feelings, which are given to the element water.

The circular and concentric lines dowsed by Ian Taylor do rather suggest that certain dewponds might indeed by used for seasonal gatherings, the villagers perhaps dancing in a circle around the pond.

With the image of the Full Moon reflected therein, this would indeed have been a powerful form of ritual. Frazer, in "The Golden Bough", has this to say :

> *"For she, too, loved the solitude of the woods and the lonely hills, and sailing overhead on clear nights in the likeness of the silver moon looked down with pleasure on her own fair image reflected on the calm, the burnished surface of the lake, Diana's Mirror"*[30].

There is also a folk tale recorded in many parts of the country about those who saw the reflection of the Moon in a pond, thought it was a cheese and tried to fish it out with a net. This may be the origin of the name "Moonraker", which is sometimes used as a name by traditional witch covens?

One of the methods of scrying is to look into a bowl full of water, to which perhaps a small amount of ink has been added, and to relax the mind. In a short time, images may be seen and one can direct attention in particular directions. It is particularly powerful, in my experience, if one can arrange so that the Full Moon is reflected in the water. The ritual of "Drawing Down the Moon" also seems strongly linked with this in that the cup of wine or water is usually an integral part and, in some traditions at least, catching the reflection of the Full Moon on the surface of the wine (the cup has to be almost full to the brim for this!) is central to the whole ritual. Rhiannon Ryall confirms this connection by stating that "at a Full Moon ceremony, a large shallow dish was placed in the Circle to reflect the moon as it was considered a link for the Drawing Down"[72], and Doreen Valiente refers to Robert Cochrane's use of the cup of wine at the full moon esbat and the importance of the moon being reflected, in this case by means of a mirror, into the wine.[85] One might perhaps therefore see the pond as a large scrying mirror where one could go to obtain enlightenment. Perhaps the established tradition of constructing dewponds by moonlight is a memory of some earlier time when the ponds were used for purposes such as scrying, midnight of the Full Moon clearly being the most powerful time for such an activity.

Whilst dew only formed a relatively small contribution to the water in the dewponds, there was undoubtedly some, important at least in a symbolic sense, and this may have added to the overall mystique. Dew is very special water with magical qualities and there are traditions of using it in order to see faeries. It is also a tradition for maidens to awake early on May Day morning (if indeed they had actually been to sleep that night!) and to wash their face in the dew. This would ensure their beauty would remain or be enhanced. Robert Graves refers to the "moon-dew" which was used by the witches of Thessaly; this was a girl's first menstrual blood, taken during an eclipse of the Moon. And Edward Bach obtained his remedies by using the dew that had settled on particular flowers: in this way he thought that the subtle essence in the flower could be transferred. And still traditionally the best way of cleaning valuable antique carpets is to leave them out overnight allowing the dew to settle on them. This power which was evidently thought to be present in dew might well have been transferred in popular imagination to the dewponds themselves, thus enhancing their mystique.

Many such places remain magical, although lack of maintenance has led to many of the ponds drying up. The pond in the photograph is a case in point. It is in a magnificent location, high up on the Yorkshire Wolds, looking out over deep dry valleys, virtually out of sight of human habitation. The photograph was taken a few years ago, however, and the pond is now dry. It is still a special place, however, and, as with many ponds, dry or not, a good place to sit and meditate or perform a ritual.

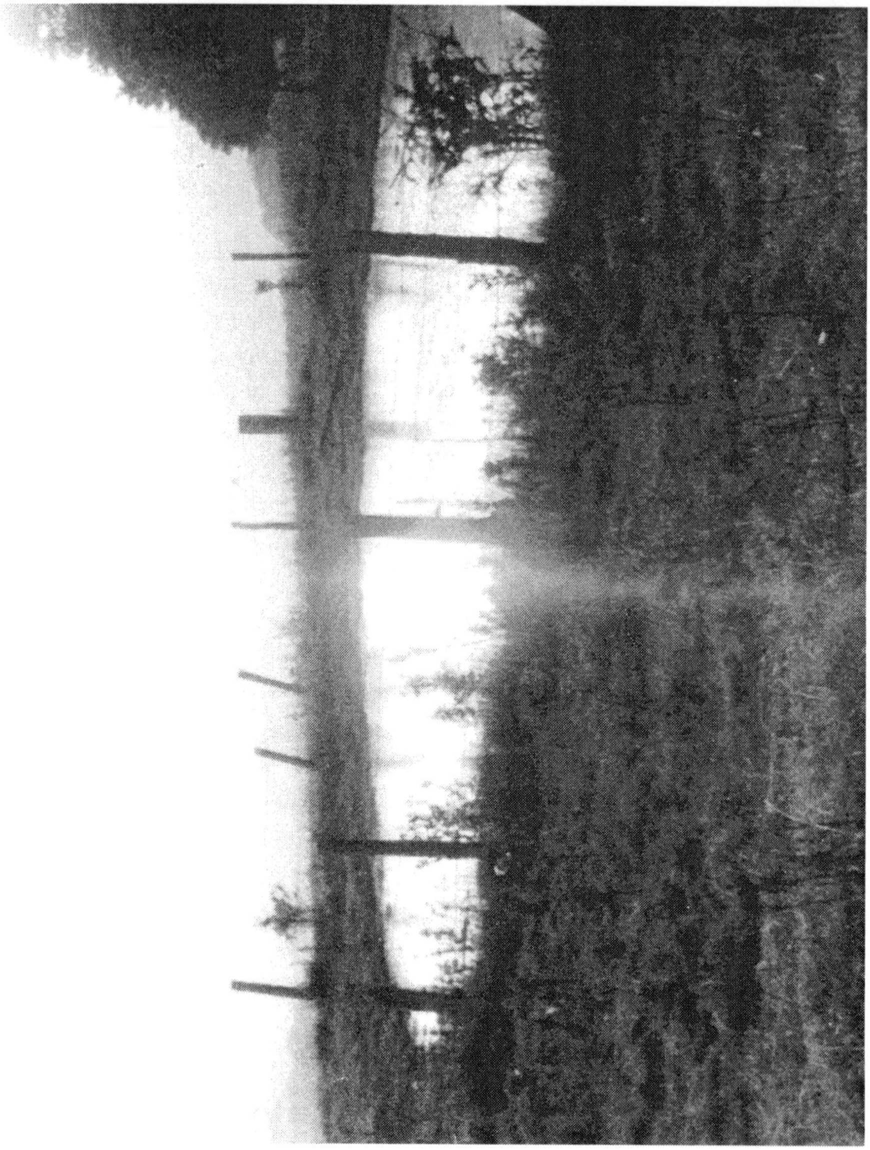

Ponds are often surrounded by trees. These help to maintain the water level by reducing evaporation. It also creates an environment different from and cut off from its surroundings. Here is a mini-woodland, a small area set aside from the needs of cultivation where the four elements all find expression - water in the pond, air moving through the trees, the earth beneath and fire in the sunlight piercing the canopy of leaves and reflecting off the water.

They are places not for active ritual but somewhere to find a quiet spot on the bank resting your back against a tree and watching. Perhaps this explains the popularity of fishing - that you can do just that, but your fishing rod and tackle insulate you from charges of being "peculiar"!

Ponds and pools are especially places where we can experience the Goddess, as in the following account by Edhel:

> "Facing the huge Fir I stroked its rough bark, which as ever gave off an inner strength and deep calm. Just beside me, a small burn tumbled into the pool. Its water's always cold and sweet. I drank, enacting a personal ritual which had become part of my visits, and listened to the soft gurgle of flowing water over rounded boulders. I yawned, suddenly tired, and for a few moments closed my eyes in deep relaxation. ... I shook my head to clear it, glad to feel the fir at my side, then for some reason looked into the water's depths, and saw a face watching me. Deep within the pool was the face of a Lady, who seemed to fill and dominate the water. Each patch of light and shade, each frond of water weed, which before had seemed just part of the pool's inner self, now seemed an essential characteristic of Her face. Slowly the Lady's face seemed to float upwards, to a position just below the surface, and Her fair hair somehow blended and merged into the reedbeds. Then She called to me! ... She spoke, but try as I might, was

unable to hear or comprehend Her, or even the sound of her voice - just the surging noises hissing back and forth. Even so, we seemed to communicate, though on a level far removed from my conscious ability to comprehend. Eventually, I was aware of the noise diminishing, seeming to dissolve like effervescent bubbles, and I became conscious of being back beside the pool."[25]

The Seashore

The line where land and sea meet has always been considered "between the worlds" and therefore somehow special and apart. It has that timeless quality deriving from the awareness that the waves have been breaking without end since the dawn of time. The cycles of the tides - daily and monthly - also makes us more conscious of time and the rhythms of the Earth.

Nowhere in this country is more than 75 miles from the coast. As a result most of us are familiar with it, from day trips to the seaside, perhaps from our earliest years. Imagine what it must be like to see the ocean for the first time, however. Standing on the sea shore, half of the view is of an immensity of water, far more than you have ever seen before.

This overwhelming presence of one element is awesome, evoking fear and attraction at the same time. It is ancient, having been here for longer than people were ever on the Earth, the hypnotic cycles of the waves having been flowing in constantly, continuously, for all that time, without a break. The beach - the strand - that narrow line between the two - and therefore somehow special, since it has that power of boundaries and thresholds that in Celtic teaching were considered so important. Constant motion. Immensity. These are the feelings that are evoked on the seashore - the solid land, the familiar, and the ever-changing waters, ever-changing but always there.

If we sit or stand near the shoreline, hearing the waves break against the rocks, pebbles or sand, it is very easy to enter a meditative state of being where we can tune in to those primaeval rhythms. We, being human, can only stand so much of this, and there will be a time when we have to get back to our more active and trivial world of things and events, when we cannot stand more of that immensity.

This feeling is well expressed in Martin Armstrong's poem, "*The Cage*":

>*Man, afraid to be alive*
>*Shuts his soul in senses five,*
>*From fields of uncreated light*
>*Into the crystal tower of sight,*
>*And from the roaring songs of space*
>*Into the small flesh-carven place*
>*Of the ear whose cave impounds*
>*Only small and broken sounds,*
>*And to his narrow sense of touch*
>*From strength that held the stars in clutch,*
>*And from the warm ambrosial spice*
>*Of flowers and fruits of paradise,*
>*Into the frail and fitful power*
>*Of scent and tasting, sweet and sour;*
>*And toiling for a sordid wage*
>*There in his self-created cage*
>*Ah, how safely barred is he*
>*From menace of Eternity.*

The seashore is a good place for a ritual. Firstly, it is relatively easy to get away from people. If there are cliffs, even low cliffs, they provide both shelter from the wind and protection from being seen. It is also perhaps the one place where a bonfire is acceptable and will not attract too much attention, particularly if the Coastguard is notified beforehand. The wonder of seeing the Full Moon rising up out of the sea is something that will long be remembered.

I have been present at several rituals on the Holderness coast of Yorkshire. The cliffs of boulder clay are eroding rapidly, but provide sheltered coves where a fire can easily be lit. There is usually a very powerful atmosphere present, but also a sense of a celebration, where a barbecue would not be out of place. It is almost instinctive to leave the fire and walk down to the water's edge, for quiet contemplation amongst the vastness of the elements before turning to see in the distance the small flickering light, evoking very primitive feelings of companionship within the vast protecting darkness.

That coastline ends at Spurn Point, which is now almost an island. Most people who visit have the feeling of it being a very special and different place to the rest of Yorkshire. The water predominates - water and sky - and one is very conscious of changing weather conditions. A friend expressed it thus:

> "I felt strange strong lunar feelings, feel cautious of the big river and the vast sea. I feel it is like the end of the world. The river and sea look welcoming but are also deceiving, deadly waters. I have had these feelings since I was young."

A classic seashore ritual where fire plays a central part is that described by Dion Fortune in her novel "*The Sea Priestess*". It involved lighting the Fire of Azrael, a mixture of juniper, cedar and sandalwood, which can be lit on the beach when the sea is at the utmost ebb, and watching and experiencing the scent of the incense until it is put out by the salt water rising tide. It can induces visions and clairvoyance to those who inhale its vapours.[29]

Doreen Valiente tells of a moving seashore ritual which took place on the night of a midsummer full moon at a lonely spot on the Sussex coast. The tide was out, and the low moon reflected a silver path on the surface of the water. Incense was burnt, and a circle drawn on the sand. The Old Ones were invoked and their blessing asked for. The help of the Moon-goddess was requested. A plaintive melody was played on a pipe and a young woman danced to invoke the Moon-goddess to permit the spirits of the sea to manifest. The music, the sound of the waves and the movements of the dancer had a hypnotic effect. As the dance came to an end, forms began to be seen over the tops of the waves, continuing until the tide came in and the ritual was closed. She says in conclusion:

> *"I was told that such ceremonies are not performed out of idle curiosity, but for a definite purpose. This purpose is to bring humans back into a living kinship with nature. Once a person has had even one of these experiences of contacting the forces behind the world of forms, he or she is no longer in mental bondage to that world. Their own elemental vitality awakens, in kinship with the rest of nature."*[81]

CHAPTER 6

SPIRIT PATHS TO HOLY HILLS

Witches traditionally met, and continue to meet, on hills, not necessarily that high or prominent, but on land that is up out of the village and not quite of this world. As Doreen Valiente says:

> "The gods of many pantheons were believed to dwell upon mountain-tops. Perhaps it is the very inaccessibility of the height itself, the effort needed to climb it, which invests it with the sense of other worlds beyond the everyday. There is a sense, too, of eternity upon heights seldom trodden by the feet of men; as evidenced in the popular saying, "As old as the hills". There, indeed, "the Old Gods guard their round", and the veil between the seen and unseen may grow thin. Pagan temples were frequently built upon hilltops; and the memory of these old gatherings and rites is often behind the association of a particular hill-top with witchcraft."[82]

John Matthews, writing of a traditional witchcraft group, says:

"They used always to meet on hilltops - to be between the earth and the sky - and because of the numen of the place, whose influence was to be felt in all that they did."[52]

I associate hills with the element of Fire, because we go up to the Sun, to view the sunrise and sunset and to light the seasonal beacon fires. Hill brows, saddles and tops all seem to be significant points in terms of relationship with the surrounding landscape and mounds, beacons, standing stones and stone circles have often been located in such places by the ancient people for that very purpose.

There is something very special about a small hill, a bit like a small island. I have dreamed about them on more than one occasion - one which had a building enclosing the very top and one where there was a holly thicket with a secret entrance. In literature, too, the small hill figures prominently. Stanley Weston Mason's story "*Kestrels over the Beacon*" centres around Arrowby Beacon :

"...a hill altogether more majestic than any of the others, and it dominates the skyline like a vast camel's hump". The beacon has, within its confines, a group of large blocks of stone - glacial erratics - and a large spreading oak-tree, near where a springlet dribbles into a pond. Each of these features and the relationship between them are important in the context of the story.[51]

The path to the top is very important, even with a small hill. Geoffrey Russell's discovery of a septenary maze on Glastonbury Tor is perhaps an extreme example of this, but there is often significance in the path to a sacred site when it involves climbing a hill. It is usually not straight up, but a curving or zig-zag route, where the turning points are places to stop, take one's breath and admire the view before continuing. They will often be points that many people have paused over the years and this will have built up a certain atmosphere about that spot which reinforces its function as a gateway or stage in the route.

It is often the declivities in a hill which are important. Indeed, witches' ritual sites on hills are often a little way from the summit in a depression which provides protection both from the wind and from prying eyes. Doreen Valiente says:

> *"I have been given an eye-witness account of how a party of people climbed a height of the Sussex Downs one night at the full moon, to contact the ancient powers. Their purpose was partly to carry on a tradition, and partly to feel, if only for a moment, that kinship with the forces of life which is the deep root of primitive religion ... It was a fine night of bright moonlight, with a strong wind, and a few flying clouds passing across the moon. My informant described the climb up the hill, and how they reached the summit already in a state of suppressed excitement. They lit their fire, choosing a slight dip in the ground so that it would not be visible to any watching eye in the village below."*[81]

One aspect of the element of Fire is that of communication and so I have included paths, tracks and roads here, as well as the places where they meet. Although ostensibly artificial, both are significant in terms of our relationship with the landscape where they are organic, arising out of the land itself. Paths are an indication that others have come this way before and, if read aright, they can be a guide to understanding the land. Even more fundamentally, we can learn from the way the path follows the landscape, as if it were a living being (which it is), something about our approach to life itself. The path as teacher is an archetypal concept which is a living reality for pagan peoples in all parts of the world, including the traditional Craft. It is "the watercourse way", as Taoism has been described, that flowing with nature which is our desire in seeking out special places in the landscape.

We leave a trail as we pass and this, over the generations, leaves a wisdom and character to each path which is unique in its quality. This applies to animal tracks perhaps even more than human paths. Traditional badger paths may be hundreds of years old and the same may well be true of other tracks as well. The sensitivity which animals possess means that their response to the Earth Spirit is direct and harmonious. We can learn a lot from looking at the routes taken by animal paths and the places they frequent.

Where two paths cross, a place of power and of spirit is located. It may have been there before the paths, but it also has a spirit which emerges from what each path separately possesses. There is an interaction of energy and character. It is a place where meeting becomes a possibility - a place to halt and change direction - a place to explore the vicinity.

Cross-roads and places where three or five lanes meet are traditionally said to be meeting places for witches. This is perhaps not surprising as they are associated with the goddess Diana Trivia, or Diana of the Tree Ways and of Hecate, the moon goddess. The significance of crossroads, apart from the utilitarian reason that they were easy to get to, was that the psychic traces left by everyone who ever walked the roads would mingle and set up some form of harmonic echo. The significance of the three- and five-lanes ends was that at least one of the lanes had to be going to the meeting-point itself, only likely if something was going on there. Doreen Valiente gives two examples of places where witches used to meet - one, in Ashdown Forest, Sussex, now known as Wych Cross, but formerly known as Witch Cross - a place where three roads meet. She also refers to the crossroads at the Wilverley Post in the New Forest, near the ancient oak called the Naked Man.82

Such places, where ancient tracks and paths meet, are still places that witches and other pagans are drawn towards. There is something very magical about such spots, and one can usually find some perfect spot to cast a circle very near the junction but which is protected from view by trees or a hedge. So often have I found such spots that one begins to suspect that they may genuinely have been meeting places going back at least several centuries.

Implicit in the descriptions I have given of places is that they exist on more than just the physical level: that there is an 'Otherworld' component which can be attuned to and visited. The idealised landscape, the dream landscape, that landscape reached in pathworking are where we can make contact with those elements in the landscape which are important to us, which have most meaning, expressing both archetypal images and things we need for ourselves. This is tied to fundamental urges which help to explain why, as individuals, we prefer some landscapes to others.

I will not add to the published guidance on visiting that 'Otherworld' directly by methods such as meditation and pathworking as well as in dreams, astral projection and shamanic journeying but will try to give a flavour of its geography.

In a sense there is no limit except that set by the imagination. But we are dealing here with an Otherworld which is archetypal in nature and to which others also have access. What elements of landscape come out if we look at guided meditation and pathworking?

Marian Green, in "*A Witch Alone*", gives us these images:

> *A narrow path through a field of wild flowers. A path winding along a hillside towards a small cluster of trees. A grove of trees - oak, ash, holly and hawthorn. A wood, a dim twilight with trees crowding closely. An arching doorway of slender rowan trees, leading to a lighter glade. A fallen tree, entwined with ivy and creepers.*[37]

Rae Beth, in "*Hedge Witch*" takes us to the following places:

> *A clearing in a wood, with green grass, wild flowers and tall trees. An escarpment looking east, with a fresh breeze. To the south, a place where the Sun strikes through the trees, in a shaft of golden light. To the west, a downhill slope and a path to a spring which feeds a small pool. To the north, a flat-topped rock set firmly in the earth. A winding downhill path to a cave, the entrance a crack between two rocks. A crystal cave, with a floor of sand. A passage winds down, coming out on a beach, near meadows, pale sand and high cliffs. A freshwater stream bubbling out of the rocks flows down to the sea.*

> *"This is a wild country, as well as beautiful. There are chalk uplands and belts of trees. Except for the highest ground, it is thickly wooded. Through tangled forest, you will emerge on a bare hillside. You begin to climb up. Once at the top, you can see for many miles. Chalk, flint and tough grass are all beneath your feet. You can*

see now that you are standing on a long ridge. This, too, is a sacred place."[4]

We can see immediately that we have encountered many of the elements that make up the landscapes we have already looked at in this book, as if they were deeply ingrained into our consciousness, as archetypes. These are the sort of places we can dream about, and it is a clue to the sort of place which it is right for us to find if we can recall our dreams for a period of time.

Of course, what we call dreams are, in fact, several different things, or rather, a mixture of several different things woven together into a single experience. One element in dreams is undoubtedly what has been called astral projection, out-of-the-body experience or shamanic journeying. In other words, there is part of us that travels somewhere at night and we experience this as a dream.

There is one area I have gone to on several occasions when dreaming. It is woodland, some of it of an open nature, some of it close and dark. There is a straight trackway leading into it from the nearest minor road, which skirts the edge of the wood for several miles, along which are isolated farms and hamlets. The wood has an area of small hills and hollows, which I would certainly recognise if I went there physically. There is also a long slope down to some lakes at the bottom of the hill which have pine trees around. Another area I have been to more than once in dreams is an area of sand dunes (some of which are quite tall), perhaps half a mile or so wide, between a coastal village and the sea. There is a track leading down from the village. These repetitive dreams are nothing extraordinary and I merely give them to show the sort of landscape which tends to well up from the depths of our being.

Another landscape of the spirit which is currently growing fast is the computer network which is being used increasingly by pagans not just as a means of communication but for ritual circles. Mark Peters describes how this can work, with pagans using the computer network to cast a circle several hundred miles wide, each participant taking a specific part in the ritual determined by where in the network they were:

> *"The truly amazing thing is that it works so well. The power raised in a circle this size has to be experienced to be understood. I think that because of the nature of the circle we tend to actually have it on an astral level more than a physical level. Which to me seems more appropriate as a place between the worlds. Perhaps the world of electrons is the place between"*

A site suitable for ritual purposes - an open lawn with large spreading oak trees within an ancient wood.

CHAPTER 7

FINDING OUR PLACE

We have looked in the last few chapters at some of the places which pagans and others, past and present, have found particularly numinous, powerful and strong in the Earth Spirit, where they have been able to experience the Earth Goddess. I now offer suggestions for finding such places yourself. Are you attracted by such an idea? If so, do you know why? What sort of place are you looking for? What would you do there?

There are any number of possible answers to such a question. We might, for example, want:

Somewhere we can go so that our spirit is uplifted and we can feel more confident in and positive about life.

Somewhere we can meditate or undertake pathworking.

Somewhere where the circumstances are most suitable for the attainment of 'cosmic consciousness'.

Somewhere to sleep to bring prophetic dreams.

Somewhere to undertake 'sitting out' or an initiatory experience.

Somewhere for intimate conversation, counselling and healing, where the atmosphere will aid the process.

Somewhere to perform a particular seasonal or magical ritual.

Somewhere to make love.

Somewhere to meet the Old Ones, the elemental beings and the beings on this plane in an atmosphere of trust.

And these are just a few of the possibilities!

If we are serious about encountering the Earth Spirit, about finding the Secret Places of the Goddess, the Enchanted Places, then we must make sure that we approach this adventure in the right frame of mind and spirit. We might not necessarily know exactly why we want to find these places and this is quite all right. We are drawn to some things in life and we don't necessarily know with our conscious mind why we find some ideas attractive. Indeed, it is highly likely that, if you are drawn to the subject matter of this book at all, you will already have made several of the steps necessary to find those secret places of the Goddess.

Looking back at my own life, I have frequently found special places where I could go and allow my spirit to soar - solitary spreading beech trees overlooking an expanse of countryside; the depths of an oak wood; a clump of pine trees on remote moorland; a bend in a stream surrounded by birch and alder; a small grass lawn surrounded by gorse bushes - all are very special to me. I remember them with affection and they all affected me deeply and enabled me to grow in wisdom. Kay Watkins feels this about such locations:

"I enjoy exploring places with an air of solitude to them. I am someone who seems to absorb other people's emotional states so I often get a sense of being in need of space away from human contact. There is definitely an emotional reaction within me when I visit special places. I suppose it's similar to how people describe going into churches. There is a feeling of holiness. When I need solace I instinctively find the right place to go; it may be a piece of wasteland where there are small groves of young silver birch or it may be a park with a quiet space with mature trees that have a sedate and noble air to them. Celebration-times are different again, going out with one or several other people to special tree-places is energising and mysterious - the 'sum of the whole group being greater than...' feeling."

So, as a preliminary, think about the times when you have been somewhere where you felt the presence of the Goddess strongly, where you felt something special about the place you found yourself, perhaps a little protective to it. What was the place like? It may have been just a small patch of waste land hemmed in by factories, a great spreading oak on the edge of primaeval forest, a hidden corner of a field or a dramatic headland on the shores of the ocean.

What did you feel? How differently did you feel from your everyday life? Did you feel any bodily sensations? Did you stand, sit or even lie on the ground? Was there a particular spot where you felt happy to be in, or did you walk slowly in a meditative state? Were your spirits uplifted? Did you begin to have a different perspective on your everyday life? What time of day did you go? Did you see or sense anything unusual, not of normal everyday reality?

The questions are endless, but the important thing is to be aware that in all probability you have experienced the sort of sites I am writing about. They don't have to be dramatic - it is enough that they are important and significant to you. Part of what you have to do is to look for and find their significance, which may not be at all obvious on the ordinary level.

It requires that state of mind (which may be called intuitive, psychic or whatever) where we can see small distinctions between things, trusting our intuition as much as our physical senses. This is the key to improving psychic ability and it is also the key to finding those sites which are special to us.

Carlos Castaneda tells the story of how Don Juan asks him to find "his spot". Using his conscious mind, he is unable to do so, and he only finds it when he falls asleep exhausted in the right place.[11] In other words, a different side of our being takes over, right brain as opposed to left brain thinking - intuitive rather than analytical.

So you will probably already be doing it, but it is always as well to go through the process of asking why you want to find a site and what you want to do there, even if the answer is a simple statement like those I give above. We may not have any clear answers but they probably centre around the feeling that we need to come closer to the Goddess and that we can do this more easily by approaching her in her own domain, where Nature is predominant and where we are aware of the changing skies. In the words of Doreen Valiente:

> "I who am the beauty of the green earth, and the white Moon among the stars, and the mystery of the waters, and the desire of the heart of man, call unto thy soul. Arise, and come unto me. For I am the soul of nature, who gives life to the universe."[27]

So the first answer is simply: "To be, because thereby we gain wholeness and strength." This "healing by place", this being close to the Goddess, in a spot where the Earth Spirit is flowing, is a strongly revitalising experience and this in itself is enough.

Actually, this can be more difficult than it might appear, as it means leaving things behind - not just physical things like camera, notebook, ritual sword or whatever, but also, most difficult of all, our preconceptions. The purpose is to experience the site as it is, in the present, neither bringing the rose-tinted spectacles of how we would like it to be nor taking away photographs or written impressions, which are at best a pale reflection of reality and at worst like trying to bring home the waterfall in a box.

Paul Devereux, author of *Earth Memory*, calls this "being and seeing", which he defines as "just being present at a site and being open to the receipt of whatever information the site might be yielding."[21] Whether we give such experiences the grand title of "meditation" ultimately doesn't really matter.

I hope to give some idea of how to find the location or locations that are the right places for you in your local area. I have emphasised the local area for various reasons. Firstly, my subject is not the dramatic or famous sites like Stonehenge, Avebury or Glastonbury: it is the less obvious - places probably not generally recognised, a little off the beaten track; places that are protected and can only be found by those with a certain attitude to what they are doing.

Also, they are places that need you. They need your love and attention and they need you to visit regularly. Only if you live fairly near is it practicable for you to do this, at different times of the day and month and at different seasons of the year. So they need to be local sites and you have to find them.

Whilst I hope to provide some clues, there is a time when you have to give yourself up into the hands of the Goddess and God and allow them to take you where they will. I put forward a way, only one of many possible ways, of finding a site, in the hope that it might generate ideas and enthusiasm.

A good thing to start with is a map of your local area. The map is a symbol, and in many cases a very detailed symbol, of the landscape. It is not the landscape, but through it, as through other symbols in magical practice, one can gain insights into the character of the land. Experienced map-readers can gain a vivid impression of the form and nature of the land just from looking at a map. I have always been capable of spending hours just sitting and looking at maps and I realise now that this is essentially the same process as meditation on some symbol or icon.

So, sit down with a map in front of you - probably the 1:50,000 or 1:25,000 sheet. Open it out to an area that you are drawn towards. Then just look at it. Don't control where you look but notice as a detached observer the features to which your eyes are drawn. Ask yourself if there is a boundary to "your area". Where does your eye keep being drawn to? Try to visualise the actual landscape - are there hills and valleys, or streams? Are there any ancient sites and areas of wood or heathland? Or perhaps there may be names that strike a chord somewhere deep within you. Don't try to analyse all this - just let it flow right through you.

You will probably find that your eye has picked out a few places for you, perhaps the corner of a wood, a hillside near a stream, or a bend in a river near a farmstead with a name that echoes through your mind. Keep these places in mind. Before actually visiting them, try to imagine what they are like. Then see if you can dream about them.

The process is, in essence, the same as any other technique for trying to dream about something specific. Before going to sleep, sit and look for a few minutes at the particular part of the map that you are interested in. Don't try to commit it to memory - just look at it - follow where your eyes lead and see if any images of the place emerge. Don't worry if they don't - keep that desire in mind - to visit that locality represented by the map - as you fall asleep. There is no guarantee of success but, after a few nights of doing this, you may well have some strange dreams of floating over an unfamiliar landscape. If you do, see whether, when bringing it back to memory, you can note certain distinguishing features that might be recognised later when you visit the place physically.

This process of finding a site or sites is not a fully worked-out intellectual course of action. It is more intuitive: it requires us to be in the right state of being - to be doing the right things at the right time. We need to keep open to ideas and information from whatever direction they may come, and this requires a certain state of mind - relaxed yet alert. We need to allow things to happen and not block them because of our own rigidity.

This is the state of mind in which things can happen - things we might call coincidence, synchronicity, "the flow" or the operation of the Laws of Manifestation. We might also call it magic. The following quotation, the origin of which I do not know, puts it very succinctly:

> "The moment one definitely commits oneself, then Providence moves too. All sorts of things occur to help one that would otherwise not have occurred. A whole stream of events issues from the decision raising in one's favour all manner of unforeseen incidents and meetings and material assistance which no man could have dreamed would have come his way."

It is also helpful to make a commitment to the Goddess at a New Moon. This can be as simple as lighting a candle and explaining what you feel that you want and asking the Goddess to allow you to become aware of things which are necessary in your search. Trust, commitment and dedication will open up currents which will help you achieve your aims.

When you are in this state, books fall open at just the right page with the information you want. You bump into somebody you haven't seen for months in the street who casually tells you something you needed to know. Things will happen at the right time: we have set the process in motion and we will know when to take the next step.

In some old witchcraft traditions the necessity of being in the right frame of mind before taking part in any rituals is emphasised. Essentially this amounts to being at peace with yourself and those close to you. Presumably, the reason for this is that if there is any unresolved dispute or worry in the back of your mind then you cannot put yourself fully into the magical working, ritual or whatever. Tony Wedd tells a story with a similar sort of feel to it:

> "Max Freedom Long was facing bankruptcy. The great 1929 depression had hit Honolulu and visitors were few and far between. He ran a photographic shop, and the lease was due for renewal. No one would buy his cameras, and he had no way of paying for the renewal of the lease. His big rival in the city had turned down the offer of his stock and equipment, for they were both hard hit. Max was hit the harder as he had a smaller, less well capitalised concern. He went to see a kahuna.
>
> The kahuna took a tumbler of water and grated a little ginger on to the top surface. Looking down into the glass, she announced that 'the door was not open'.

The situation is translated into a visual picture. Max Freedom Long was not getting through to his god because of a block, though the exact nature of the block was unknown to him. The kahuna bade him go away and punish himself in three ways: fasting till midday, cutting out his cigarettes and making a generous donation to some charity:

> *After paying his 'forfeit', Max Freedom Long returned to the kahuna, who looked into her glass again and assured him that the door was now wide open. "What do you want to happen?" she asked him, and he suggested that his troubles would be over if his rival would buy out his stock for $8000. After checking that this was a reasonable figure, the kahuna came up with the advice that he should list the stock in detail on paper, and on the following Tuesday at 2 o'clock call on his rival, put the inventory quietly on his desk and go away. When, after half an hour he returned, his rival would accept the proposition ... By carrying out instructions exactly as told, Max Freedom Long came to a good end instead of financial ruin."* [89]

When you feel the time is right, go out to one of the places you found on your map, always remaining open to last-minute changes of plan. I call this "dowsing with your feet" but again it is really an attitude of mind.

Dowsing, sometimes known as water-divining though you can find anything with it, is a way in which that deeper, wiser part of you that knows things because it realises it is a part of the universe can communicate with your ordinary conscious self.

Traditionally the dowser used a forked twig of hazel, although nowadays angle rods made from the wire of an old coathanger seem to be more popular. Actually, you don't need the rods - it is more convenient just to imagine that they are there. It works just the same!

The technique is to keep in your mind what you want to find, whether it be water or buried treasure, and to walk along until you are standing over the point being looked for. The deeper part of you will cause the muscles of your hand to move imperceptibly but sufficiently for the twig or angle rods held in a position of unstable balance to move. That is really all there is to dowsing.

I am suggesting something altogether more instinctive, which you probably do anyway. Imagine that you are walking along a path through a wood. The path forks. Which direction do you go in? Don't think about it - just do it. Walk slowly along the path that beckons you - you will know which one it is. Walk slowly, with a regular rhythm, as quietly as possible, but relaxed, so that your body is resting on your legs - let them take all your weight. Feel fully grounded. Allow your hips to move freely with each step. Experience the place with all your senses.

You may come to a natural halt at a certain point. What were you thinking about? What is there at that point that made you stop? Perhaps you feel led to walk off the path into the wood itself. Is there something there that you feel may be a sign to indicate which direction you should go in? Again, follow instinctively where you are led and you will find your place. If possible, fall into the frame of mind where you know that coincidences are going to occur and there is significance and meaning in each twig and leaf, bird flight and puff of wind. If you can keep focused on what you want and sensitive to what is happening within and around you, then you will know what to do.

Actually, it is not usually as simple as that. You are going on a sort of trial or test, where there will be false trails where you need to retrace your steps. You may get stung and scratched and muddy or fed up with the whole thing. If you can flow with these feelings and see them as part of the way towards what you are seeking, you will come through. It is like the bee trying to escape through the glass of the window that is open at the bottom. If it would only relax and sink down to a lower level it could get out, but it is seduced by the view of freedom through the glass.

Of course, you can use the same technique when cycling or driving a car, subject to the necessary concerns for safety and respect for other road users, or even at a bus or railway station in deciding which bus or train to take. The important thing is to make decisions on the spur of the moment, or rather to stand back and see where you go, or end up, always keeping sufficient consciousness to find your way back again.

"Selene" gives a vivid account of the unpremeditated act of finding a site:

> *"Once I had broken away from the others, I found myself crossing a little footbridge set over a small drainage ravine, going straight into the heart of the wood. The forest around me was absolutely still, I had left the noise and people behind, and felt unaccountably but unobtrusively excited the further I went. I experienced nothing of the classic case of panic one is supposed to encounter when one approaches or enters the Realm of Pan, but felt drawn on as if something I had been missing and longing for within myself was waiting for me just ahead.*
>
> *I came to a clearing through the close press of trees and saw myself standing in a vaguely circular space, and I*

Distinctive trees which are markers for a special place - twisted thorns in an area of ancient woodland

knew I had arrived. There was a suitably atmospheric ground mist swirling round my legs, and a slightly gloomy shaft of clouded-over sunlight illuminating this clearing. I just stood and absorbed the 'charged' atmosphere, drawing it to myself with sighs of relief, and for welcome moments I basked in this special sacred place."[73]

Psychic Questing is a phrase that has come into use in recent years, mainly due to the efforts of author Andrew Collins, although the principles on which it is based are very ancient indeed. We are not the first people to tune in to the Earth Spirit and visit special places in the landscape. So, when we do go to those numinous spots, we may well tune in to those who have gone before.

Psychic questing covers a very wide range of activities but is centred on establishing psychic contact through the landscape with the past. This may involve the retrieval of artifacts or helping on a psychic level to achieve the resolution of some unfinished action. It relies heavily on the operation of accurate psychic ability and synchronicity and many examples are given in Andrew Collins' books of where remarkable items have been uncovered with the associated occurrence of appropriate events.[15]

For example, a friend of mine was led to dig in a clearing in a wood and immediately unearthed a witch's wand wrapped up in a cloth. It was obvious what it was and he put it back again and covered it up, because he knew it had been buried deliberately. The relevance of psychic questing is that its reliance on intuition and a strong relationship to the landscape are both equally significant in seeking out those special places which are right for you. We may not have been the first to frequent such spots.

A friend once presented me with a four-leafed clover she had spotted a few paces ahead as we were walking across a field. Her eyes had been drawn to it out of the many thousands of clover plants along our path and she was able to go straight to it.

Afterwards she told me the secret of finding them, one part of which was that you mustn't be looking for them! This has to be genuine: pretending not to look for them doesn't work!

Adapting this principle to looking for sites, we could perhaps say that you are most likely to find them when you are not looking for them. In this form, the statement is very harsh. We can, perhaps, put it in another way. We need to get to know an area - we may well come across an actual location quite 'by chance' when we are not looking. In a sense, these places will come into your life at unexpected moments. They may indeed be places that you only visit once but the one thing they seem to have in common is that they come unexpectedly - unannounced.

It is quite possible for your chosen site to be very close to "the beaten track". Indeed, I know more than one site which is adjacent to one of the network of Long Distance Footpaths established by the Countryside Commission and therefore at certain times has its fair share of walkers and ramblers. There is, however, a difference between a summer Sunday afternoon and midnight of the Full Moon in February, for example.

Surprisingly often, sites can be found just "off the beaten track" - places people don't go because they don't lead anywhere, perhaps a bend in a river, an isolated valley or just off a path in the corner of a wood, field or forgotten piece of rough land. With regard to appearance, your site may be quite striking in its landforms, trees or other features, or it may seem quite ordinary to anyone else. Often, particularly if you are on a path, there may be a change of direction, or three or five paths meeting. Perhaps a change of slope. Very often there is a special tree which you will recognise again. Or nearly always a small patch of ground a little way apart from but related to the path. There may be a change of level - somewhere set apart by height as well. Trees can actually create such a form, perhaps by being the centre of a sheltered area, some having branches that enclose a protected area.

But it is your relationship to the site that is important. It often has that quality of enabling you to see without being seen, and I have also found that there is a strong sense of place and the feeling of being the centre of the universe. You may need to go back to the vicinity a few times before you find a precise spot. This can be a ritual act in itself.

CHAPTER 8

ENTERING THE PRESENCE

What happens when you find somewhere?

Well, first of all, you stop walking and stand still: this is usually the first stage. It is a sign of recognition of some quality in the place which demands that you linger. This may be all there is to it - to catch one's breath, look at the view or examine some feature more closely. What these sites have in common is that you feel you have reached somewhere. It is a definite place, different from those through which you have been walking.

Refreshment may be taken - perhaps a drink of water or an elaborate picnic. Elizabeth Kent shows very vividly how picnic sites are part of this picture:

> *"Finding the right picnic spot is not always as easy as it might appear. Trollope ... insists that 'a picnic must be held among green things. Green turf is absolutely an essential. There should be trees, broken ground, small paths, thickets and hidden recesses. There should, if possible, be rocks, old timber, moss and brambles. There should certainly be hills and dales...' In David*

Copperfield, Dickens describes a picnic which takes place in 'a green spot, on a hill, carpeted with soft turf. There were shady trees, and heather, and, as far as the eye could see, a rich landscape.'[44]

The picnic is special - at its best it really merges with the sacred feast which may be held at the seasonal festivals. The picnic site becomes for a time a home and takes on an aura which lasts long after the physical picnic is over. Trollope's criteria for a good picnic site would apply equally to somewhere intended for meditation, ritual or making love. We are reminded of the prospect/refuge theory of landscape aesthetics and the requirement of a site to provide the circumstances to allow us to "see without being seen".[1]

Perhaps it is not the sort of thing one often talks about, but I often feel the need to piss, to use an old but appropriate word. I experience this very much as a sacred act linking me with the place. In the time that it takes, I find that I can enter a particular state of mind very easily. It may have something to do with the release of the muscles of the bladder and the consequent effect on more subtle levels, perhaps related to the base chakra.

It is certainly linked in my experience with a relaxation of some of the muscles in the anus and a definite tingling in the perineum, that area between the anus and the sexual organs - this tingling is often accompanied by a feeling that some desire is actually attainable.

Perhaps it has its origins in sexual feelings but in my experience is linked with that collection of hopes and aspirations which astrologically are linked to the Midheaven - what we are aiming for in life. I am sure that in terms of subtle energies it is linked with the base chakra and the stirring of energy up the spine, which is known as raising of the kundalini. It is also an indication that the location you are in is special in some way, though it may not necessarily seem special to anyone else.

The creative process can be released at locations that are a little bit "out of the way". I think this is a question partly of being away from the mass of people and therefore one's aura can expand to a much greater extent than in 'normal life'. We are also less affected by random 'thought waves' which, whether we are conscious of it or not, are constantly bombarding us. One of the reasons why I suspect witches met (and still meet) at remote spots at midnight is that most people were likely to be asleep and so they were less affected by thought waves from individuals going about their daily lives, the rather different thought waves from individuals who were asleep or dreaming being less disruptive. This may not be conscious, but the resulting atmosphere is most definitely different in quality, being stiller and more concentrated.

Access

Another important consideration is that of access to potential sites. Most of us live in towns and many don't have ready or easy access to the countryside, for financial or other reasons. Do we need to go into the deepest countryside to find our site? Not necessarily. Indeed, the emphasis in this book on local sites embodies a recognition that there are problems involved in getting there, and therefore the more local a site is the better.

Most of us live in towns, but how well do we know them? Richard Mabey has drawn our attention to what he calls "The Unofficial Countryside" in his book of that name.[50] By this he means the considerable areas of land in built-up areas which are habitats for wild plants and animals. They are perhaps a little bit out-of-the-way and need some searching for, but there are probably some such places within relatively easy reach of most of us.

Old railway lines, embankments and cuttings, canal towpaths and the banks of rivers and land drains are likely places, as are the corners of fields and hedges that often survive even when surrounded by industrial sites. Looking from a tall building in any of our towns and cities will confirm that there are far more trees than we think. What we are looking at are the interstices of modern civilisation, where Nature can gain a foothold.

I found one site whilst attending a Pagan conference recently. During the lunch break most of those attending preferred to stay inside the building (admittedly it was raining!). I, however, ventured out, beyond the playing fields surrounding the school to the far corner where a small footbridge led over a stream to an adjacent wood. Here, on the edge of the stream, where the field boundary changed direction, was a small group of hawthorn trees. Moving through a narrow gap, I found myself in a small enclosed clearing with a grass floor, perfect for a ritual.

These places can be as full of the Earth Spirit as any in remote countryside, particularly at times like sunset and the night of the Full Moon. If you take the trouble to find them you can make them your own. By your actions they will take on added significance.

These places can be very vulnerable to "development" and the growing pressure to recognise the importance of "urban greenspaces" - wild areas of value for people of all ages as well as wildlife - is something which should be supported in whatever way we can.

Near where I live, within easy walking distance, was a small triangle of land between a railway embankment and a filled-in drain, along which there was a path. The land itself was wild and there were some large trees as well as more open land. I used to go there and stand looking at the starry sky as well as getting my life into some sort of perspective. That land is gone now - all the trees have disappeared - they've built flats there, and something has been lost - something I can now only recall in my memory.

Mériém Clay-Egerton recalls a similar experience in her childhood which affected her very deeply:

"One day I went to the woods as normal and, horror of horrors, all that was left was a mass of torn up ground, and tattered scraps of branches and leaves. I experienced a terrible crying surging lament for all the life that had perished. Here the presence or essence of the woodland hung like a reproachful miasma over the torn remains. I was told by adults that the land had been sold to developers to build houses on. I have never been able to cry physical tears, but that day I felt totally riven apart, and realised like those who had lived and loved innocence was no protection against the madness of men, and their addiction to money. Neither beauty nor life was of any use in a world where blindness was a ripe fitting companion to destruction."[13]

Elsewhere, she describes another wood which no longer exists, buried under the concrete of an airport runway extension. And yet it does exist, for her, in her memory. She gives a very vivid account of the place because, as she says :

The surviving remains of a guardian thorn tree now intertwined with an elder growing nearby.

The wooded slope down to a sacred spring

"I know that only in my mind can I walk the ways in which ghost snakes can still sunbathe alongside basking sand lizards."[13]

Some of us have particular problems with access and these need to be addressed. Physical disability and visual impairment, even when coupled with the freedom which a wheelchair or guide-dog offers, can limit the extent to which remote sites can be visited and certainly may make us more reliant on others. However, it is surprising how many suitable locations can be found that are not far from public roads, car parks, bus stops or railway stations.

I don't underestimate the problems which many have in getting there in the first place, but places can be revealed which are both possible to get to and out-of-the-way at the same time.

Other disabilities may be less obvious but nonetheless real. For example, the quality that we often seek in these special places is that of solitude, but the other side to this is vulnerability to danger. Women particularly feel this and if the fear of possible attack, for example, is too great, it can be debilitating and any benefits to be derived from visiting such a site can be negated.

There are partial solutions to this. You may feel safer if you take a dog, a bike or even a horse. There may be the option of going with someone else, perhaps allowing them to retire to some distance away so that you can experience the sense of being on your own and yet know that there is a companion within calling distance if you need them. "*Finding Your Way in the Woods*" is a short but very good booklet which has some useful things to say about the matter of danger and fear. The first is to accept we are afraid, of both known and unknown dangers. This seems to arise partly because what we are doing is both meaningful and powerful to us, and to some extent it can be a vital part of what we are doing. It has also been mentioned to me that having a sense of purpose helps to reduce fear and that one can feel less vulnerable at a remote site if one feels one is there for a reason and has something specific to do.

There is, lastly, the legal question to be addressed. In contrast to such countries as Norway, where there is a right to roam on any uncultivated land, in Britain we can be accused of trespassing, and this makes it important to be clear where one stands morally on this issue. In practice, because of the sort of places which I go to and the times of day when I go there, I have never been stopped by a landowner or their agent. My personal inclination is to feel that the remnants of wild primaeval forests, moorland, heaths and other uncultivated land cannot be morally 'owned'. There may be individuals who have responsibilities and duties to that land (and that, of course, includes ourselves) but that is not the same thing as preventing others from entering that land, unless there is a very good reason. Some nature reserves are closed at particular seasons to avoid disturbance to breeding birds, for example. Nevertheless, one often feels more at ease on land owned by public bodies such as the Forestry Commission or local authorities, for example. It is a matter of judgement in each individual case. Ultimately, if you trust in the Goddess, she will protect you and, seemingly, make you invisible to prying eyes.

Sites for All Seasons

Pagans are very aware of the cycle of the seasons with its reminders of the continuing process of life, death and rebirth and the importance of living in the present. The year is seen as a wheel, turning with the seasons, with key points in the

Julian's Bower, a turf maze

cycle as times of celebration and communion with Nature, the Goddess and the God. We rely on Nature and seasonal rituals emphasise that we are all part of the cycle of life. As well as the solstices and equinoxes, most pagans celebrate four other festivals, often traditionally known as Candlemas, May Eve, Lammas and Halloween, although the equivalent Celtic names of Imbolc, Beltane, Lughnasadh and Samhain have recently become popular.

You will probably find that you will visit more than one site in the course of a year, each having its own changing character, and perhaps one will call you at one season and one at another. This is natural and a positive response to the changing seasons and you will instinctively choose the right place.

At Lammas, I have visited the edge of a birch wood adjacent to the wide expanse of a wheat field about to be harvested and having a clear view out to the August Full Moon low in the southern sky. For Samhain, a beechwood feels right, high up on the hills above human settlement with an open windswept feel, a carpet of fallen leaves and the sound of the wind through the branches. For Yule, perhaps a site on a hillside with a view out to the setting midwinter sun, close to a patch of old holly trees. A secluded grass lawn, surrounded by hawthorns, might be just right for a May Eve celebration, and so on. You will find that your own seasonal cycle and your growing awareness will help you to find suitable places.

Boundaries, Gateways and Guardians

The journey, the approach to the site, is part of the total experience. This may often take place in silence as if mentally and spiritually preparing oneself. The concept of pilgrimage comes to mind - that process, often on foot, of visiting a sacred place, which has implicitly the idea that the journey itself can be as significant as the destination. Worthwhile goals may not always be achieved without a trial and this is often true of a sacred site. You will probably have reached your site by a roundabout route. This may be absolutely right and, indeed, it tends to be in the nature of the way to a sacred site, as symbolised by the path of the labyrinth.

The intricate pattern made when following the path of a maze, one of the names for which is "The Trip to Jerusalem", induced in those threading or dancing it a certain state of mind. Rhythmical turning and the experience of coming close to the centre only to swing out again, can be a powerful experience if undertaken in the right circumstances. One of the claims for the maze or labyrinth was that it could very quickly induce that state of mind which might otherwise only be accomplished by a long pilgrimage.

Kim Taplin quotes John Cowper Powys, who describes a certain spirit which can be entered into when walking:

> "... the field-dung upon my boots, the ditch-mud plastered thick, with little bits of dead grass in it, against the turned up ends of my trousers, the feel of my oak-stick "Sacred" ... the salty taste of half-dried sweat upon my lips, the delicious swollenness of my fingers, the sullen sweet weariness of my legs, the indescribable happiness of my calm, dazed, lulled, wind-drugged, air-drunk spirit, were all, after their kind, a sort of thinking, though of exactly what, it would be very hard to explain."[77]

When walking along a well-worn path or even an infrequently visited trail we can, if attuned in the right way, be aware of others who have walked the path before. This seems to be because as we walk along we leave a sort of 'psychic trail' which can be picked up by those who are particularly sensitive to such things, perhaps by such techniques as dowsing. An old path will have memory of everyone who has ever walked along it deep within its subtle body. We can see that this will have its effect on us at a very deep level. Old trails to sacred sites, old pilgrims' ways have over the years built up in this way a powerful and tangible 'atmosphere'.

The route you took when you first discovered the site may not be the way you feel you want to approach it on subsequent occasions. Perhaps there are several different possible routes which you may feel inclined to take at different seasons of the year. Even after you have visited it many times, you may feel it is right to approach it from a particular direction, perhaps varying according to the season. You may want to follow a contour, a stream or animal track. These latter can be quite striking at times, as Tony Padfield recounts:

"She got to the first stile, and as she stepped down a Hare got up from under her feet and dashed into the field. It followed a regular little beaten path, almost straight, that led into the farther woods... she rose and moved to the edge of the wood. Here the rain fell harder on a windswept landscape - but the Hare paths were clear, luminous in the silver light... She set off on the Hare paths. They took her directly and easily; her feet pattered effortlessly instead of sinking in mud."[61]

After a while you will get to know your special route and the stages that you come to. They will take on a significance such that the journey to the site is an important part of the whole experience.

Certainly it will help you to attune to the spirit of the place. The thing that seems to emerge is that there are stages on the path, sections of the journey that seem to prepare us mentally, spiritually, perhaps physically, for the site itself.

Allen Watkins, with particular reference to the mark points on the Old Straight Tracks, or leys, makes the point that they fit very well being classified into the four elements and that the leys could well have been used for initiations into the Mystery Traditions. He asks: "Was the ley ever used as a ritual? It is so perfectly fitted for such use that it is hard to believe otherwise."[87]

What might have been true for the straight track was undoubtedly true for certain other paths. In some traditions, the path is in reality a learning experience, whereby certain wisdom is imparted at certain points on the path. This may be related initially to certain inspiration or revelation that occurred at a specific location. Its subsequent use as a spot for teaching gradually reinforces its significance. Joined by the path, these spots or stations for teaching were viewed in pre-literate cultures in the same way as the idea of serial vision on a walk through a city - a complete system of learning from the landscape itself, without the intermediary of books and other teaching aids that we have today. Learning from a path through the landscape is an archetypal concept which has, with growing literacy, been almost entirely forgotten, though it is a common theme in certain Taoist teachings. As John Michell writes:

> "... the Australian natives make ritual journeys in the steps of the gods who created the landscape, every feature of which commemorates some episode in cosmogony and has also some present significance for human or animal life. A rock may mark a source of fertility in women, a tree the place from which a certain animal or plant is generated. Each station on the journey has its day of the year, its mythological episode,

the rituals and songs appropriate to it and its properties useful to men or animals."[53]

Particularly when we leave the path and walk over rough ground or especially through a wood, there is a very striking phenomenon that I have often noticed coming into play. When I am in the right frame of mind (perhaps something to do with brain waves or a slightly altered state of consciousness, perhaps brought on by the rhythms of steady walking, as we have already seen in the quotation from Powys) my steps seem to be guided. I know just where to put my foot and I flow past obstacles - patches of mud, nettles, branches of thorn trees, etc. It seems as if I am in tune with that deep part of me that knows just which path to take, where to stop, where to look and where to go. Tony Padfield seemed to imply this when he referred to walking along the hare paths, and Mériém Clay-Egerton recounts a similar experience: "The brambles seemed to part as if a knife were cutting butter. Nothing rejected me, no whipping branches, no feet pullers, nothing"[13]

It is likely that you will sense the presence of a place guardian, which may have both physical and Otherworld components. One of the indications is that you will stop briefly, perhaps to catch your breath or look at the view. What seems to emerge naturally like a spring bubbling from the ground is the need to ask permission to continue. This is a deeper permission than that of the legal owner of the land: in essence it is the permission of the site itself. Whilst this is usually given willingly, it is important to take this asking permission seriously. "No" means "no" and, at least on that occasion, you should turn back. Otherwise, the act of asking becomes a mockery.

Often you will find your eye drawn to some feature in the vicinity - very frequently it will be a tree which is distinctive

An indicator of the magical quality of a place - holly growing in the split trunk of a thorn tree.

in some way, perhaps by having a double or triple trunk, by having another tree growing close to it, such as "The Two Lovers", a beech and pine which grow together on the summit of Crichel Down in Dorset.[91] I have seen a thorn tree growing out of a willow and a small thorn growing between the roots of a large oak. The tree may have a hollow between its branches where water may collect. The bleeding yew tree in the churchyard at Nevern in Pembrokeshire is not the only example and it is worth looking out for. It is a question of looking at things with an eye to the unusual - to seeing behind the surface appearance to the essence behind. In more hilly landscape, there may be a rock that embodies the spirit of the place guardian.

You certainly get human or animal guardians of some sites. They can appear apparently from nowhere - the woman taking her dog for a walk, the old retired farmer or even the young child. The exchange is usually pleasant enough - though you are aware you are being checked up on. Then, if you have passed the test, some information is imparted, unbidden, which is often just what you needed. It is a strange occurrence, but one which has happened so often that one almost looks out for it.

The animal guardian can also be striking - a wild animal, perhaps a deer, owl or hare, that comes surprisingly close and looks at you for longer than seems natural - again, the sense of checking up, but accompanied by a definite sense of real communication at the deep non-verbal level.

The spirit lying behind form (what Rupert Sheldrake calls the "morphogenetic field") consistently brings through particular archetypal shapes, whether it be in rocks, trees, human faces or more temporary forms such as running water or clouds. This can result in what is known as 'simulacra' - natural forms resembling other natural forms - so that, for example, there are cases of hills resembling women's breasts (such as the Paps of Anu in Ireland), faces hidden in rocks or tree trunks, etc. This is one of the ways the nature spirits can manifest to us - by taking on the mantle of some natural physical form and revealing themselves through it. As John Michell says: "The eye is naturally inclined to anthropomorphize, and so too is nature".[54]

Perhaps there may be nothing obvious physically at all, but the presence can be felt and perhaps very precisely located at a particular spot. Sometimes the vegetation at these localised spots may be different in some way - a lush patch of clover, for example. Sometimes, there is a small patch of bare ground. The tradition of spots where nothing will grow is very well established. Probably the most famous of these is Dragon Hill at Uffington in Berkshire, where there is such a patch of ground. The legend is that it marks the spot where St George killed a dragon: neither grass nor anything else will grow at the spot where its blood was spilt. And at Burn Butts, in East Yorkshire, there was by tradition a bare patch of ground, formed either by a farm labourer who used to stop and pray at that spot every day or because it was the site where a man was attacked and killed.

These places where nothing will grow suggest some form of localised energy anomaly and I have certainly known strange effects on vegetation following rituals. It would seem that any strong emotion, particularly if associated regularly with a particular spot, might well induce permanent or long term effects on the vegetation of a site, either by encouraging more luxuriant growth, the favouring of certain rare species or, as in the examples given here, of denuding an area of any growth at all. Sometimes this may be related to "fairy rings" or the localised "hot spots" of radiation that the Dragon Project research in Oxfordshire found coinciding with particularly lush patches of clover.

It is as well to linger in the vicinity of these site guardians, tuning in to them and noting your impressions - getting to know them. They do have a function, and to attune to them is important in ensuring that your journey further on will be harmonious.

Having been allowed through by the site guardian, our approach can become more intense, focused - we are aware of being on holy ground. As Guy Ragland Phillips says:

> *"...where one approaches any numinous place in open country - a summit, a grove, a well, a river source or a place rendered sacred by people in the past - it is appropriate to take off one's shoes as Moslems do in the mosque."*[64]

To illustrate a walk to a sacred site, I give my own account of the path that leads to what I call the Valley of the Druids:

> *"I leave the motor road high up on the open Wolds, and take the chalk and flint surfaced green lane. The woods crowd in on me as I make my way along the ancient track. The energy paths of every being which literally made their way along here before me have permeated the very fabric of the earth and my footsteps are well guided indeed.*
>
> *I pause a moment beside an ancient grove of beech trees, tended no longer now, though their presence and calm remain. Here, perhaps, within living memory, the ancient rites were enacted and may yet be again. The trees will stay in readiness for that time.*

Waters flowing from a series of springs in a sacred valley

At the top of the dry valley I scramble down to the green path, following the old hedge of thorns and elders, pointing the way, beckoning me onwards as I descend the gently curving path down the rolling hillside. The path runs through scrub or low woodland and then begins to rise a little.

Here I approach a very definite gateway which for me is strongly associated with an Otherworld guardian. To the left, the hedge changes direction and thus marks out an uneven rough uncultivated area which, for me, is a numinous site. At the point where the hedge changes direction is the stump of an old hawthorn. Much of the trunk has broken off now, but I remember it in its prime - a powerful guardian of the site beside whom I always stopped and exchanged a few thoughts and feelings. The Guardian is still there - new shoots are springing up and I still acknowledge her presence. It is very natural to stop and talk to this old wise tree goddess and to listen to her. She has never refused me access to this site, but I hope that if this did happen I would listen and obey.

The hill edges in more closely. Instinctively I take off my shoes and feel the springy grass beneath my bare feet. Past more bushes now, I stand for a moment on the edge of a sacred area, which I share with the rabbits for which it is home. I am also conscious of a silent harmony with all those - past and to come - who have touched the beauty and inspiration of this place.

Onwards now down the narrow sloping path under the hillside trees, down, scrambling to the valley bottom; then, turning back, to make the last gentle descent to the small chalk cliff. I kneel down and drink from the renewing, strengthening, sacred spring.

All is silent - the sun is set and as the branches of the woodland trees reflect in the gentle water of the pool I feel the whole of existence draw closer around me as my capacity for description dissolves into an experience of the infinite."

Your site will have boundaries. In some cases, you can, in time, draw these fairly precisely, particularly the 'gateways' - places round the perimeter of the site where it seems appropriate to enter. I remember a solitary rowan tree high up on the Northumberland moors, a line of tall beeches alongside a green track over the Wolds, an old holly tree with a massive girth on the edge of a patch of old woodland - all seem to me to embody the guardian of the adjoining sites. The word 'sentinel' springs to mind - watching over and caring for the site and opening up or closing down the site to potential visitors.

Most usually if we approach in the right spirit there is a warm welcome - the Earth likes to be visited. But I remember one dark wood on the night of an early summer Full Moon when the answer was an emphatic "No!" It was not unpleasant but, for whatever reason, I was not welcome on that occasion. I turned back.

I will conclude with and commend the wise remarks of Marian Green. After emphasising that setting up a circle in your garden need not attract the attention of your neighbours, she says:

"The same applies to the wild places, the woods, the fields of remote farmlands, the moors or the shore of the sea at night. Unless you advertise your presence by destroying trees or lighting fires and frightening livestock, no one will notice. I know, I have carried out

ceremonies in all kinds of places and no one has ever complained or written to the papers about it. If you ask Nature herself to suggest a good place where you can meet her - and sit still long enough to hear the answer - she will provide a suitable location that you would never have thought of. It will be safe and secret, so long as you wish it."[36]

CHAPTER 9

INBREATH - EXPERIENCING THE SACRED SPACE

We have all had the experience of getting to know another person - our first impressions, the sides to their character which are revealed as we get to know them better, and how we never really know them completely - we are always being surprised.

Nobody can prescribe in great detail the stages by which you get to know somebody really well and it is, of course, the same with a location in the landscape.

Meeting each other fairly frequently under varying circumstances helps in a human relationship. The equivalent is visiting the site often, at different seasons of the year, during the day and at night if possible. The site is alive, and alive in many different ways just as we are: each encounter therefore will be different. To quote from *"Finding your way in the Woods"*:

> *"It is very important that you do visit some sites fairly frequently so that you become more familiar with the lie of the land, the other people that use them, the wildlife and the sensations, moods and events which you can find there."*[2]

Although it sounds a bit formal or cold, there is a series of exercises which may prove helpful to you in getting to know your site.

The simplest exercise of all is just to find a spot that feels right to you and sit down facing the centre of the area. Make sure that you are reasonably comfortable, perhaps leaning against a tree or bank.

Then relax: don't try to do anything, not even to meditate. Just be aware of what is happening by using all of your senses.

Follow your eyes and see where they want to go, perhaps following the line of a tree branch or a faint animal track through the long grass. Allow the site to "make an impression on you" by following the movement of your eyes rather than trying to direct them.

Then, when you feel the time is right, close your eyes and listen - to birds singing, insects flying - the sound of the wind in the trees or raindrops falling - perhaps the fall of water over rocks or emerging as a spring from the hillside. And then the human sounds - the distant aircraft which, perhaps paradoxically, can only be heard when one is in remote countryside so that it actually becomes, by association, a sound which is characteristic of such a place.

If possible, don't try to name these sounds - just allow them in and experience them as pure sound. The reason is that in this way you will be able to experience them directly without the intervention of our artificial classification of the universe by means of the naming of things - useful in many ways, but for the present purpose it actually gets in the way.

Then get up and start to walk around the site. If at all possible, do this barefoot. Don't have any particular objective in mind - just see where you get to. See where you turn and instinctively walk back in towards the centre. In this way you will be able to define the boundaries of the site - at least on this occasion, for they may vary over time.

Are there places where you feel like stopping, to examine a tree or path or view more intently? Remember where they are. Be conscious of how your experience of the site varies according to where you are.

The views - the aspects - of the site will vary, but do the sounds vary? Close your eyes at different points in your perambulation. Is the sound of the wind greater at certain points? Are there spots of quiet? Do the scents vary? Are there patches of a particularly aromatic herb, or a tree that exudes a resinous vapour?

And what does the ground feel like underfoot? Are there soft, damp or muddy places? Patches of long grass? Or areas of sharp stones, nettles, thistles or brambles?

Then, using your intuitive senses, ask yourself what you feel about the site on this occasion. Does this feeling vary in different places? Where do you feel most comfortable? Most elated? Happiest? Note and remember. Find the spot that you most want to be in at the moment and stand, kneel or sit.

One of the keys to psychic awareness is to become aware of and sensitive to subtle distinctions. One exercise is to practice noticing these subtle distinctions within your site. It will help you to get to know it better.

Stand in the middle of your area. Make sure there are no obvious obstacles round about. Close your eyes and turn round a few times to try to confuse your sense of direction. Take two or three paces forward. Kneel down (still with your eyes closed) until your face is a foot or so above the ground.

Open your eyes, taking care to look down, so that you can only see the small patch of ground directly in front of your eyes.

Look at this patch, for however long it takes to take in all the details that you can see. Is it bare earth or rocks? Are there plants? Look at each stone and plant. You don't have to be an expert in geology or botany to notice things like shape and colour. Feel them if you want to.
When you have familiarised yourself with this little patch close your eyes again and stand up. Turn round a few times and take two or three steps. Turn round again a few times and then open your eyes.

You now have to search for your patch of ground. This may take some time or you may be able to go to it straight away. You will recognise it when you see it.

You may like to mark it in some way, with distinctive stones, perhaps, or a stick. Each time you come back to the site you can go to your special patch and see how it has changed since your last visit. No one else knows that patch as well as you do, and this will help to link you to the whole site.

We can continue the process of getting to know a place, by allowing it to work on and affect our senses. There is no hurry in this - it is best to take your time, keeping before you the desire to be so in harmony with Nature that you attain a state of union with the Goddess and the God. This may happen in an instant or it may involve a process of exploration and unfoldment before we and the site can open up to each other sufficiently to allow this to take place.

We can experience the site fully by means of our senses - scent, feeling, sound, sight and psyche - and celebrate the joy to be derived from them and learn how they can be heightened in an outdoor setting in the realm of the Goddess.

We experience through our senses and it is through that experience that we can get to know the Old Ones - by so intensifying that experience that we are fully in the present. It is a central part of all old philosophies that a key to living with the flow of the universe is to live in the present. Most of the time we don't do this - we are taken up with "past regrets and future fears", as Keats put it, and forget that, in the words of George Fox, "there is no time but this present". To live constantly in the present is to slow down the flow of time. Children have the natural ability to live in the present - we tend to lose it as we get older, as we remember how long a year seemed when we were young.

Scent

"Fresh air" is one of the archetypal "good things" of life, albeit one that is threatened by various forms of pollution. Even in the city, the air of early morning has a freshness which is almost intoxicating, when the exhaust fumes of the previous night have settled and have yet to be replaced by new emissions.

This early morning "window" is a reflection of the still relatively unpolluted country air, though pollution respects no boundaries and even the Scandinavian pine forests are suffering from acid rain. Most of us spend a relatively small amount of our time each day out of doors and so we do not experience that very special quality of fresh air.

The experience of walking through woodland, for example, is very much tied up with the scents associated with the place. Each plant has a scent. Some are obvious, like the resinous aroma of pinewoods, the powerful wild garlic on a woodland floor or the beautiful perfume of the honeysuckle which can pervade a night walk along a woodland path. Some are very subtle and only reveal their delicate influence when gathered together in large numbers. The bare earth, particularly after heavy rain, fungi on decaying branches and a whole host of unidentified scent sources also make their contribution.

Indeed, it is rare that only a single scent is present: it is in their combination that the characteristic aroma of woodland, for example, resides.

When wind blows past any plant, it picks up some of its essence and mingles it subtly with the essences of all the other plants in the vicinity and the aromas emanating from the bare earth and ground cover to produce an unmistakeable perfume. This is indeed a most appropriate word to use, because the skilled perfumer blends perhaps a hundred essential oils together to create something which is unique and very special.

What is happening in Nature is something infinitely more subtle. Even in a small area of woodland there is a vast number of different species, all of which contributes to the whole. Also, the scent varies from any individual plant according to its own stage of maturity and other factors such as the weather and time of day.

Of recent years, the practice of aromatherapy has become very popular. It uses the essential oil distilled out of a wide variety of plants. The use of these oils, usually in diluted form, for massage or inhalation has been found to have therapeutic effects. Many are from trees, plants and herbs which can be found on any ordinary woodland walk, although there are some from all corners of the world.

Scott Cunningham has used the phrase 'Magical Aromatherapy' to describe the deliberate admixture of resins, spices, aromatic herbs or essential oils in order to produce a definite effect on the subtle body, for healing or magical effects, or changing consciousness.[20]

Incense has been burnt since ancient times for just such a purpose by creating an atmosphere, as with the Fire of Azrael which Dion Fortune refers to.[29]

Whilst resins, spices and aromatic herbs were some of the earliest things to be transported around the world, most ordinary country people would mostly use what was growing around them.

From ancient times, it has also been recognised that aromas have an effect on the subtler parts of ourselves. Mirov and Hasbrouck, for example, write:

"All of us get elated and emotional as we stroll through a pine grove on a hot summer day when the old trees fill the air with their pungent fragrance. Big bonfires made of pitchy pinewood have a peculiar mystic fascination. As we sit watching the sparks going up, and as we inhale the fragrant smoke, we are inclined to become philosophical or to sing nostalgic songs ... Longfellow wrote beautifully of 'Piny odours in the night air'. We are all poets when we are in the pine woods."[56]

It is certainly clear from our own experience how the scent of the land, particularly after heavy rain, affects our emotions and, despite some very good artificial incenses and perfumes, this can never be reproduced satisfactorily indoors. The medical herbalist Paul Baines drew attention to the subtle effects which aromatic substances can possess when he pointed out that the alchemists considered the essential or volatile oils to be the "Sulpher or Soul" or the plant, representing its character or consciousness, and speculates that the subtle exhalations from a plant, including molecules of its essential oil could pass into the atmosphere and exert some influence.[39]

To be aware of this helps us when we are out in the woodlands and the landscape. As we breathe in the fresh and aroma-laden air we can visualise how it is affecting us, not just physically but also on the subtler levels. The scent emanating from the trees, herbs and other plants in the vicinity is part of our total experience of the place and, as such, will affect our state of being.

As an exercise, you might want to close your eyes, wandering about your site noting how the scent changes at different points. Can you notice one aroma predominating or can you detect a mixture? Don't worry if you can't identify all of them by name. Make up your own names for them until you do. Remember, they don't know themselves by the names people give them! What effect does the aroma have on your feelings and spirits? Then open your eyes and try to find the source of some of the scents. This may well involve crawling about on hands and knees!

The following trees and herbs immediately spring to mind as having very distinctive scents: Apple, Bay, Broom, Chamomile, Cedar, Cypress, Garlic, Honeysuckle, Hyssop, Iris, Juniper, Lilac, Lily of the Valley, Meadowsweet, Mugwort, Pine, Rose, Wild Thyme, Yarrow. Try to locate some of these and see what effect being in their presence has on you. This will give a clue to their magical function. Again, no one place will have the same combination as anywhere else, and this will vary according to the time of day, season and weather conditions, as well as from year to year. It is really only by getting to know a site really well that this becomes apparent.

It is interesting to note that some plants, such as apple blossom, can't be made into an essential oil and can therefore only be experienced fresh, preferably as a living plant, which therefore means going out to where it lives. The contrast between the aroma of an essential oil and the scent of real outdoor location can perhaps be likened to the difference between pure vitamins and minerals and the subtle combinations which are present in wholefoods. It is in the subtle interactions and combinations that the magic lies.

Taste

The Taste of the Outdoors? Certainly things taste different outdoors, and this is one of the reasons for the popularity of picnics. Victor, in Nick Warburton's radio play "*A Grove of Straight Trees*", puts it thus:

> "This is the way to eat bread, Guy - out in the open. You get the full freshness of it, don't you? ... It's where it comes from. From the fields to the bakery, then back out here. Close to the ground, like this. It tastes!"

Elizabeth Kent says:

> "Fresh air is the picnic's greatest asset. Its revitalising effect on appetites and food causes both to improve dramatically. Like pulling rabbits from a hat, anything produced from the picnic basket seems like a miraculous culinary feat. Everything tastes exceptionally good, better than it ever has done before. And the same meal, eaten in the Bois de Boulogne, Kew Gardens and at Land's End, will taste different each time."[44]

I will always remember the mug of tea which Tony Wedd gave me to drink whilst having a break from digging for an ancient track in the corner of his field in the remote Kentish countryside. A strong mixture of Indian and China tea, drunk in the open air - a truly new experience for me!

Many rituals include a feast and it is very natural indeed to share food and drink after what might be a very profound experience. It helps to ground you and to draw you closer to each other.

Feeling

Feeling may perhaps be our forgotten sense, but it is also our most basic. In modern society we are often embarrassed about feeling, trying to cut it off with layers of clothing and constricting ties, belts and laces. We feel with our skin, or with the nerves located just beneath it, and in order to give it a good chance to work properly we need to uncover it - in other words, to go naked, or 'skyclad' as the witches say, or at the very least barefoot. If we do so, then we will feel the air and the ground. We can also feel the weather and the seasons more fully, even if this means the cold and the wet.

I have often experienced the walk over fields and through wild woods to some secret sacred site, perhaps with a companion in the old ways, sometimes perhaps with several. Having prepared the site for the coming ritual we, almost instinctively, remove our clothes. No longer, if I ever did, do I feel in the slightest bit embarrassed by this: it is merely the final part of the preparation. But immediately I take off my clothes, a great joy seems to surge through me. Even the slightest breeze can be felt on the skin - there is a freedom which is impossible to describe to those who have never experienced it, but, above all, there is a feeling of rightness. In this natural place, all I am doing is removing those trappings of civilisation for a brief period and draw closer to the beings who surround me in that natural site.

Making contact with the ground in our bare feet does literally ground us. Life is not always a bed of roses, however. If we want to be more in tune with and closer to nature, we will also experience the thorns, stinging nettles, hard twigs and stones under our feet! It can be uncomfortable, but it is a way of getting in touch with your site. Walking (carefully) about your site barefoot, getting to know what different parts of it feel like under foot is a good exercise.

I am reminded of A.A. Milne's observation that I have already quoted about Gill's Lap, that it was "the only place in the Forest where you could sit down carelessly, without getting up again almost at once and looking for somewhere else."[55] It might therefore seem a particularly suitable place for a barefoot ritual.

I remember walking up the last part of Midsummer Hill in the Malverns a few years ago on Midsummer Day, which was very hot. Instinctively I took off my shoes to feel the warm close-cropped grass. Only on the very summit did the warm breeze begin to be felt. My link with the Earth through my feet seemed very real and fitting.

I also remember a cold January night: it was Full Moon and approaching midnight. I also went barefoot: the ground was frozen and I could not keep my feet on the ground for more than a few seconds at a time. It was not a sensible idea: I quickly saw the error of my ways and put my shoes back on! Guy Ragland Phillips has this to say:

> *"The main thing is to practice touch, practice it assiduously, cultivate the sense, use it to communicate with your fellows, with animals, with plants, with rocks and stones and the earth with which we are one. Gradually you will re-establish the lost contact with Nature; you will find that you talk to, and are talked to*

by, the trees and the wind, the sea and the stream, the leaf and the stone."[64]

As Kahlil Gibran says in *"The Prophet"* : "...Forget not that the earth delights to feel your bare feet and the winds long to play with your hair."[33] When we walk or dance barefoot we can see it as massaging the Earth: she will usually welcome it and respond warmly.

Sound

Sound is the province of the musician, but it is also a very special character that outdoor spaces have - that interaction between the sources of sound and their echoes. This quality of echo, from bird song at dawn in open woodland, and the occasional cry at midnight from the undergrowth, all provide a sense of openness which can never be reproduced indoors. Such sounds have a real effect on us, making it easier to enter that magical state. Doreen Valiente points out:

> *"The sounds of a waterfall, or of the waves beating upon the shore, tend to lull the conscious mind into the borderline state of reverie. In this way, the perceptions of the inner mind can rise to the surface, and convey their message to the seer. Natural magicians of all ages have attuned themselves to listen thus to the sounds of nature".*[83]

Jimmy Goddard has observed that the sound of wind in the trees, the flowing of a stream and a roaring bonfire all have the same frequency.[39]

These are also all sounds which tend to induce the state of mind to which Doreen Valiente refers. The harmonic combination of such sounds can have a powerful effect, as Bob Dickinson reminds us:

> *"Many a time I have walked in the neighbouring church grounds aurally locating the sound of the distant well, shifting my focus to the sound of the wind blowing through the tops of an adjacent circle of Scots Pine, then merging the two together in a synthesis of natural sound to create a powerful aurally based sense of place."*[22]

Robert Graves, in *"The White Goddess"*, says "one meaning of inspiration is listening to the wind in a sacred grove"[35] and we may in time grow sensitive enough to tell the difference in the wind blowing through different species of trees. Thus the unique combination of species in each sacred grove could give it its own special sound, if we could become sensitive enough to hear.

This sense of place is very sensitive and can be very highly developed, particularly in people with sight impairment.

Bob Dickinson has written of interacting with natural sounds at Aysgarth Falls, which I quote in Chapter 5. He also tells of the guardian of a well who, by moving the position of certain stones and pebbles, can change the tone of the running water, and refers to a piece of conceptual water music written by John Nash in 1974, the directions for which read: "Tune a brook by moving the stones in it."

The essence of all this is that the subtle interplay of natural sounds can affect us and can help us to enter altered states of consciousness. Moving around our site, sensing how the sounds change according to where we are, and how they are different again each time of day or season that we visit, will help us to come closer to the place.

Light

Light is the medium of the painter, and it is to landscape painting that we look for an appreciation of the effect of light on land - the constantly changing interplay of sun, moon and clouds and the elements that make up the land. To visit or perform rituals in the landscape is to open up to these changes - the living character of light in the land and its effect on us.

Light is in large part a function of cycles - the daily cycle of the sun through dawn, midday, dusk and night - the monthly cycle of the moon - from New Moon, waxing to Full and then waning back to the Dark of the Moon - and yearly cycle of the seasons - the dark winter and the long days of summer.

Dawn and dusk have been recognised as powerful times. The Celts saw them as boundary points between day and night and therefore both dangerous and powerful. Astrologically they are times when the Sun approaches the Ascendant/Descendant axis and the possibility of relationship with the outside world is strongest.

In my own experience, and I know in that of many others, there is a power present at dusk which is tangible. Particularly on a still evening, as the sky gradually changes colour following the setting sun, there is a change in the whole feel of a place, no doubt partly to do with animals and birds going to sleep but it also seems a time when the veil between this world and the Otherworld is thin. Nature spirits can be seen if one knows how to look and, just from being there, one feels a sense of belonging.

The time of sunset is a boundary time - a time of balance - a magical time when decisions can be taken that have a real effect on future events. It is symbolised by the green flash - that moment just before the disc of the sun finally disappears below the horizon when it turns green - fairly rare and only ever really seen over the sea, but a reminder that sunset is something that can only be experienced outside, not indoors within the confines of a room.

Beyond sunset, the landscape is still quite light, the gradual enclosing dark coming at different speeds according to the season, and at certain latitudes in Scotland in the summer it never gets completely dark. This period, which we call dusk, is one where magic is very near the surface, where that spirit which lies sleeping deep within the Earth during the day awakes and pervades the landscape. It is a time for magic and imagination (essentially the same word) and it is a time to make contact with elemental beings and nature spirits.

Moonlight is so much a part of paganism that it is difficult to conceive of it without. It symbolises so many things, but shows that there is another way of looking than the everyday. It is a window into the Otherworld. The monthly cycle from New Moon through to Full Moon and back to the Dark of the Moon is well known to pagans, symbolising the living nature of being, that constant change that we can attune to. It reflects the menstrual cycle and our own emotional cycles.

But it is the direct experience of the Moon which is primary and a central focus of pagan expression. The joy on seeing the narrow crescent of the New Moon in the evening sky after days of absence is uplifting. Seeing the Full Moon rise at dusk, large and golden in the eastern sky, when it seems so close and so powerful. And the bright Full Moon at midnight, casting shadows as if a form of day. Things look different in moonlight. There are different values to things. Symbolic actions can have a powerful effect. It is the realm and time of the Goddess and she can show you things under a Full Moon that would remain hidden in the waking hours.

Experience is primary, and the purpose of this book is as a signpost directing you towards that experience - to go out under a Full Moon to those special places and know directly. But we can talk about these experiences. The phrase "altered states of consciousness" is frequently used, and our consciousness can truly be altered in the moonlight - we think differently - more laterally - and different things are important. Things become possible under the light of the Moon that are not under the bright light of the Sun.

Moonlight is particularly powerful when reflected in its natural element, water, and a bowl or pool of water can become a strong scrying instrument when used in this way, as mentioned in Chapter 5.

Psyche

Experiences at dusk and by moonlight are very characteristic of what we might call the Psychic sense. We have seen in Chapter 2 how the psychic or magical sense arose from the essential unity which is at the heart of the universe. Thus the psychic sense underlies all the others. We may not be consciously aware of it most of the time, but it is giving us a lot of background information, impressions and feelings all the time.

The Earth is a living being who has many levels of awareness. Just as we have an aura and chakras and energy flows in our body, so does she. If we want to experience this, then we would do best to go to those places where her subtle body energy - the Earth Spirit - is strong and experience her with the subtle part of our own being.

There are many ways of encouraging the psychic sense - many organisations and magical orders offer development groups. There aren't many good books, but one is "*Your Psychic Power and How to Develop it*" by Carl Rider[70], which is a lot better than you'd think from the title.

Essentially, to open up the psychic sense (and any of the other senses incidentally!) we need to be still, stilling the body but also stilling the mind of ideas and the spirit of yearning to be anywhere other than where you are or any time other than the present. This last is probably the most difficult. Then you may begin to discern the hidden meanings behind outward things - the sound of the wind and bird song, the shapes made by leaves or twigs. They are providing the raw material for the subconscious intuitive mind to work on, far more than is available in any indoor setting.

The principle behind "Altered States of Consciousness" is a relative one: some things will encourage a change in consciousness and others will make it less likely. What we have to do if we want to enter such a state is to build up the former and try to avoid the latter.

We know already what some of the factors encouraging a change in consciousness are: to be present at a location where the Earth Spirit can be most powerfully felt, such as a sacred spring, rock outcrop or primaeval forest (places that Paul Devereux has called "The Mind-Gates of Gaia") and to be present at dusk or midnight, particularly at the Full Moon. If the place and time are right, then it may be very easy to enter the Otherworld, particularly if combined with one or more of the traditional ways of achieving such a state, such as meditation, fasting, dancing, rhythmic drumming, incense, ingestion of psychoactive plants and sexual ecstasy, or, more likely, a combination of these. In the Northern Tradition, there is the practice of "sitting out", about which Nigel Pennick has this to say:

> *"The spiritual exercise tradition involves 'sittings-out', postural exercises, and, most of all, inner discipline. There is no need for images and elaborate ritual. Knowledge comes from within, illuminating the outer world. Utiseta or sitting out is an important technique, where a person 'sits out' under the stars to hear inner voices and commune with the universe. Spiritual exercises such as Utiseta are practices designed to bring the aspirant into communion with ultimate reality. ... Suitable locations for sitting out are high places of ancient sanctity, preferably those away from populated areas. ... Solitary, wild places, especially those known to be sites of ancient numinous quality, geomantic places of power, where the flow of önd is appropriately strong, are ideal."*[62]

All we can do is to "set the scene" and allow that part of us that is in tune with the deeper levels of the Earth to come through while our everyday mind is stilled. Then we will see things and experience things that are beyond my words to describe.

Moments will spring up that will be remembered for a long time, when we seem to be seeing more into the essence of things, when we are conscious of other beings, animals and plants as 'our friends' - part of the same wholeness - such that we can communicate with them. We become much more aware of what is happening and what is going to happen, even from moment to moment. We feel, in the seconds that such a state lasts, that it is "doing us good" at a deep level - we are being healed. We also feel a certain power - we know we can achieve things, and it is up to us.

These feelings, which I have tried to describe, however inadequately, are very different in quality to those I have had indoors. There is a sense of vastness but also of belonging.

There is a joy which is strange. In "*High Magic's Aid*", Gerald Gardner describes it movingly:

> "'nay,' said Morven, 'I think you will never advance, if you feel not the old secrets of joy and terror 'tis useless for you to go on.'
>
> 'I would go on,' said Jan, 'I felt things which seemed to brush against my soul, how was't with you Thur?'
>
> 'I know not, but there seemed there was some mystery of worship, delicate, but as a dream, the queer thing is, I can scarce remember what happened, I was as if in a trance, but I think of it with joy.'"[31]

Attuning to the nature spirits and elemental beings is best done by letting the site teach you itself, in its own time and in its own way. You may not see the nature spirits, but you may be able to experience them through the other senses. A good guide is how you feel. It is good to keep them in mind, consciously sending out positive thoughts and feelings towards them. They will certainly be aware of this and of your motivations. Your actions of dedication, tending and ritual will all help to build up a relationship with them. When you do become aware of them it is a marvellous feeling of warmth. Morgan Raven provides some guidance on this:

> "When you're first attempting this form of communication, you'll find it much easier to start off in some place which is remote from human affairs. Find somewhere where humans have made as little impact on the environment as possible. ... When you've found your starting place spend a few minutes on meditation. This will help to ensure you're in the best psychic shape

for your communication attempt. Then sit quietly thinking about what you are trying to achieve. Open yourself as fully as you can to the world around you. Let down all your defences - physical, psychic and magical. When you first do this the first sign that you are getting anywhere will be a deepening sense of anxiety, even fear. This will cause you to tense up or even snap your defences back up. Try not to do this and instead try to relax into your fear. You're actually being put through a test so that the spirits can find out whether they can trust you enough to reveal themselves to you. Try to let the fear wash over you like icy water off a dolphin's back and let it flow away. ... If you are able to let the fear decline and wash over you, you'll find yourself in a state of stillness. ... Try this technique as often as you wish and gradually the spirits will become more used to you and you'll become more aware of them. You'll become aware that there are several different types of being ... You may begin to hear certain noises which herald the arrival of these beings or even faint whispers at the very limits of your hearing. You may find yourself led by one means or another to a special place of power for you where you can go for spiritual or magical recharging or where it is easier for you to contact the spirits."[67]

I remember a Lammas ritual I was taking part in at a site we had not been to before. We consciously sent out a welcome to the spirits of the place. Before long we all became conscious of a presence surrounding us and a white mist enveloping the ritual circle. It was not unfriendly, certainly curious but positive. On this occasion, the low light levels actually seemed to be used by the elemental beings to show themselves to us. Indeed, this can form the basis of a useful exercise - an exercise in imagination.

The best thing to do is to find somewhere in or adjacent to a wood and go there at dusk, as the sun is setting and the place gradually going dark. Sit or stand somewhere comfortable. Look towards a tree or mass of bushes - somewhere dark and getting darker as the sun goes down. Feel the stillness and anticipation of dusk as the birds quieten. Look slightly out of focus - see if you can notice what look like individual particles of light moving rapidly around.

Get yourself into the frame of mind where you acknowledge the presence of the nature spirits and other beings, even though you might not be able to see them. Then start to imagine - imagine that you can see them in the shadows - what would they be like? Build up a picture in your mind and then release it. The nature spirits will be conscious of your presence and they can manifest through the shapes that your mind imagines in the gathering dark. Just allow this to happen - and don't be too surprised if you begin to see things. Just accept them as normal.

There are human spirits as well, as I know from experience, which Evan John Jones has called "The Hidden Company":

> *" ... not so much seen as felt and partially seen: the hazy forms that seem to be part of the working but are out on the rim of the circle. ... it is not a personal contact through one person. Nebulous and ill-defined though it may be, the presence of the Hidden Company is one that is felt by all and recognized by all. In this sense, the Hidden Company are perhaps the guardian spirits of the coven."*[43]

I will finish with an apt quotation from *"Finding your way in the Woods"* :

151

"By the time that you can give an interesting guided walk to a friend for about an hour without getting lost, running out of ideas or getting tangled in the briars and stung by nettles with wet feet then you are starting to tune into the Glade"[2]

CHAPTER 10

OUTBREATH - RESPONDING TO THE SPIRIT

Having said in the opening chapter that I wanted to show paganism as inclusive rather than exclusive, I want now to concentrate a little more on actions which are specifically pagan. It is therefore addressed both to practising pagans from different traditions and to those for whom this is all a new experience. My intention is that there will be something here that everyone can build upon.

We have looked at ways of experiencing the site, of getting to know it, feeling it. This is fine and may be sufficient but at some stage it is quite natural to feel that something more is needed - that some response to the spirit of the place is needed.

What do we do when we visit our special place?

One answer, and quite an acceptable one, is that we don't have to do anything: our very presence, in the right frame of mind and spirit, is enough.

It is Paul Devereux's "being and seeing", although even that may be too active. Gautama Buddha sat under a bo tree until he saw the morning star and gained enlightenment.

I am reminded of the tale of the old Yorkshireman sitting on a bench who was asked by a visitor how he spent his time. "Well" he said at last "Sometimes I sits and thinks, and sometimes I just sits." Perhaps we could all do more "just sitting". Actions on our part should really have the aim of achieving a greater integrity with the place. Looked at in this way, we can see that they are not indispensable: it is quite possible to just sit. If so, this is fine, and you will know.

However, for many of us, symbolic acts can help to achieve this integration. I have called them ritual, which perhaps provides a wider context than usual, and it should be emphasised that this is not a book on ritual as such.

Instead, I attempt to look at some of the elements from which ritual can be made up, rather like an artist's palette - a large stock of possible actions to be used as appropriate in any interaction with the spirit of the place. I particularly emphasise those elements which are relevant in an outdoor setting.

Flexibility and responding to the spirit of the place are key concepts here: the ritual should be place-led. There is no room for the cut-and-dried rigid set formula. This denies the life spirit which is such a central tenet of paganism. The elements we shall be looking at and our use of them are derived in large measure from the place and our instinctive response to it.

Ritual can be constantly adapted to circumstances, by which I mean that we can interact with the site as the ritual progresses, so there is "feedback" as it were. Whereas our front room is unlikely to change significantly during the course of a ritual, an outdoor site will do, whether it be from the gathering dusk, a shower of rain, gust of wind, the cries of animals, flight of birds, flurries of falling leaves, blossom, twigs or snow - all give life to a site and, if we are attuned to the deeper levels, can reveal their meaning to us, just as, in a more extreme way, the meaning of the runes was revealed to Odin after hanging upside down in a tree for nine days and nights.

Just as we experience the essence of the site through our senses, we express ourselves through our various faculties of voice and movement. The place itself will be a reflection of time and we need to be aware of this - of the season of the year, phase of the moon, time of day and weather conditions. Each of these will affect our own being and therefore will affect what we do. We can, however, bring our artist's palette, which has been charged with colours from many sources: tradition that has been handed down, information in published writings, contacts with others, and inspiration, either spontaneous, or arrived at through meditation, pathworking or dreams.

Tending the Site

A major theme of many old traditions is the importance of seeing things as they really are, and one of my aims in writing the previous chapter was to encourage people to experience their site as it is. In building up a relationship with a site, this is what we have to do.

It is generally considered that any human relationship stands a greater chance of flourishing if one partner accepts the other for what they are and is not always trying to change them. The same seems to be true with our relationship to a landscape site. It may not be the same as our idealised archetypal site (which may not exist anywhere in physical reality) but it is real and we can get to the heart of reality by experiencing it to the full.

Our relationship with the Goddess is not to change her but to be changed by her, and the implication of this is that we should not interfere with the sites we visit in any way - we are merely observers.

The Goddess works within us as well as in Nature, however, and we can potentially be her agents.

The old tradition of tending comes to mind in this context. Ancient sites, perhaps particularly sacred groves, may need some attention in order to survive and survive well. Although information about it is by its nature difficult to obtain, I have been told that such features in the landscape as sacred groves, holy wells and the like often have human guardians, the responsibility of caring for the site and doing what is necessary to protect it and ensure its survival being passed down in particular families. Such a responsibility is accepted as "the right thing to do" and is carried out as a natural part of life without a lot of outward fuss.

I am not necessarily saying that in all cases there was a body of people who were aware of the significance of these special places, though the witches kept a lot of the secrets throughout the ages. Rather, it could often have been an almost instinctive behaviour which would only have been lost with urbanisation on a large scale and the consequent lack of concern for the landscape which is only now, slowly, beginning to be restored. Just as such traditions are dying, so it may be necessary to take on such responsibilities more consciously.

What might such actions consist of?

Well, for a start, we can clear litter, and I don't think anyone would object to that - to clear litter on a regular basis is a life-affirming act.

Purely practical tending in terms of keeping the right trees and plants growing well and excluding the others is, I am sure, an important aspect, in other words "weeding". Kay Watkins illustrates what can be done:

> *"I sometimes go out with the intention of visiting a tree, a bit like visiting a friend. When I visit friends it can be for different reasons depending on who the friend is, and it's similar with trees really. There was a beech tree that I discovered probably about three years ago when I was walking the dog on some waste land. It wasn't easy to find because there were brambles, nettles and elder growing all round it. It was a young adolescent and I thought it looked a bit stifled so next time I went that way I took some secateurs and gloves with me and cut a few elder branches and brambles to give it more room. I discovered the parent beech tree that time so I felt like I was visiting a family after that. I always have to give the tree a slight touch when I first get there and then I hug it and always lay my face against the bark. I get a feeling of calm when I experience the coolness of the bark and the roughness on my skin."*

There is also a less immediately tangible side to tending, and that is the effect on the site that comes from our visiting and performing ritual. The site, the land, the Earth Spirit, the Goddess respond to our care and concern and the site becomes more alive as a result. The Goddess likes to be visited. These sites which are strong with the Earth Spirit welcome those who come in the right frame of mind. Something mysterious happens when we enter the presence of the Goddess, and neither we nor the site are ever the same again - we are both changed as a result.

It is natural to express affection and love, and so it is when we meet the Goddess in her own realm - we give offerings and words but, as with human contact, it is by embracing her that we can come closest. Massage is very efficacious for relaxing tensed muscles - it is also very enjoyable. We may liken dancing to massaging the Earth with our feet, and to think and feel in those terms is good if thereby we realise the significance of what we are doing.

I think when one goes beyond this one needs to be aware that we do not legally own the land. Some landowners are cooperative and will welcome our efforts: others will not. As we noted in Chapter 8, we may well be trespassing, and we therefore have to be particularly clear and sure that what we are doing is morally right.

The general principle with tending is to know what you are doing and to do as little as possible. A few examples will do to illustrate some of the principles involved. The sacred springs and holy wells are being clogged up, because of the lowering of the water table and provision of alternative water supplies. Many of them are being forgotten about. As Edna Whelan and Ian Taylor say:

> "Local people, once the guardians of these places, have become preoccupied with other concerns and many - in fact most - Holy Wells and Sacred Springs are the victims of neglect and, occasionally, abuse."[90]

Many landowners will be happy to allow a spring to be cleared - this is a potential meeting point between the orthodox and the more esoteric side of things. Laurence

Golding gives a vivid account of what the initial freeing of a spring can be like:

> *"I had to climb a barbed wire fence to get to the puddle. It was where the spring came out of the hillside. Probably in rainy times it flows quite vigorously; today, however, it was still, and covered with duckweed.*
>
> *I knelt down and swept away some of the weed - the puddle felt more like a pool. I cleared a little more. Pulling away some sods at the edge of the pool I discovered a rough stone wall, and in a couple of minutes revealed the well; an exquisite half-oval, about a yard across.*
>
> *I was now quite involved and scooped out the mud and leaves and sticks in the pool until feeling at last a piece of wire. It required a tug to dislodge it from the mud, and then it slid out like a splinter; a piece of rusty barbed wire no more than fourteen inches long. It was the only man-made obstruction in the well, and when it came out it was followed by a wake of tiny bubbles. I expected the water to quickly settle but it didn't; the bubbles continued. The well was set free."*[34]

There are times when ritual can be a prelude to practical action, as the following account by a pagan group in East Yorkshire to celebrate Earth Healing Day at a holy well site indicates:

> *"... we began by placing flowers and offerings on the neglected well-house, then decorated the elder trees above it. The circle was marked out carefully to avoid harming the many young frogs found in the damp*

places around the site. The circle was marked with bird-seed.

A chant and circle dance were used to raise energy to awaken the site's guardians for its protection and for us to attune with its spirit. Sally the dog proved the most psychic of the group, barking loudly when the power was at its height and a response began to be felt. Sally is normally a very quiet dog not given to barking.

The working was fixed with a visualisation and rune song. Afterwards we enjoyed a pleasant picnic in the sun."

The ground surface where a circle is to be cast or ritual performed can be a problem, particularly if you go barefoot. An otherwise ideal site may have thistles, stinging nettles, sharp stones, uneven ground, etc. which make it uncomfortable dancing, to say the least.

Before doing anything, you must get the permission of the spirit of the place, but often the judicious and regular pulling up of nettles etc. within the defined area seems acceptable, as might the sensitive levelling of the ground, burying or removing the sharpest stones, for example. It is important not to make this too obvious to the landowner or the casual passer-by: it has got to look natural when you have finished - the aim of several schools of landscape design!

Cutting back an invasive species is a valid conservation technique, but it is really for the landowner to carry out. Certainly wait a long time in getting to know the site before doing anything and learn appropriate techniques from such bodies as the British Trust for Conservation Volunteers.

When it comes to new planting, I would err on the side of extreme caution. Certainly, wait a long time before doing anything at all. Be sure that you want to do it ... and that you know why.

Between the Worlds: Casting the Circle

Whilst it is true that pagans do not generally have specific buildings in which to perform their rituals, their equivalent is the magic circle - that place which is "between the worlds" and which allows us more readily to make contact with the deeper/higher realms.

It is, of course, a sphere and it does not have to be marked physically - it is a mental creation. However, in the landscape there are many more opportunities to mark the circle in an appropriate way than there are indoors. Of course, some marks are already there. The fairy ring is perhaps the archetypal "magic circle", created by fungi growing out in a regular ring and showing by a change in the grass within it, being more luxuriant for a time but sometimes creating a bare patch. Some are claimed to be 700 years old and, since they are traditionally supposed to be witches' meeting places, you could do worse than choose a fairy ring for your ritual site, provided the location seemed otherwise suitable. Roe deer sometimes form a circle by running round and round chasing each other. I saw one in the depths of a Lincolnshire wood: it was perfectly circular, about 9 feet across, the traditional size for a ritual circle. The vegetation had been worn away to bare earth. Much attention has in recent years been given to 'crop circles'. Whilst most have undoubtedly been what I call "works of landscape art", it is possible that some simpler forms may have been caused by some atmospheric phenomenon.

A Lammas ritual held in the midst of a crop circle, a summer celebration in a circular deer path or a May Eve rite in a fairy ring would in their nature be very powerful.

161

A tree marking one of the cardinal points of a ritual circle

I do not propose to go into the practical ways of actually casting a circle, since a variety of ways is given in several books on paganism and witchcraft. One traditional way of marking the circle is pissing at the four quarters. This is a very sacred act, but may originally be linked to the way certain animals mark their territory.

In woodland particularly, trees can be used to mark, or indicate, the circle, each representing one of the cardinal points, if it can be so arranged. In such a case there is not the precision that there would be with an indoor circle - it would probably not be precisely circular, depending on the positions of the trees and the form of the land - it is a more dynamic, living and spontaneous shape.

If there is a need to mark the circle physically in some way, then this can be done with twigs or flowers or, perhaps better still, with birdseed. This has the advantage that not only is no damage done to the site but no evidence is left of the ritual as the birds will remove it for you. It can also be thought of as an offering.

When a circle is properly cast in the landscape it is not hidden on the psychic realm - indeed it can, with repeated castings, become something of a "psychic lighthouse". It will certainly attract the elemental beings in the locality and there will be a point in your ritual that you will become aware that you are not alone - you are being watched. This is not, certainly in my experience, in any way frightening, but rather comforting - they have come to observe and to welcome. Some are able to see them clearly, others perhaps as an enveloping mist, some as sound and some as a clear feeling of presence.

When a circle is cast, it becomes our temporary home. It is a very powerful feeling if, in certain rituals, one leaves the circle and walks some distance away for some purpose. On turning round, to see the circle in the midst of the enveloping dark marked by faint flickering candlelight is to feel very strongly that it is home and our place is there and that we must return. It is perhaps some faint reflection of the feelings of the astronauts on the moon seeing the coloured Earth in the immensity of space, or the small boat returning to the lights of the harbour.

Relating to the Landscape

When we cast a circle, we mark the four cardinal points. They have a great and very direct significance when we perform ritual in the open air. Indoors, we may have to use a compass or street map to find them. Out in the landscape they take on much more than symbolic reality. They have a strength which is revealed in the great cycles of Sun, Moon and stars.

The north is the direction in which lies the point in the sky around which all the stars revolve. The south is the point in the sky that the sun occupies when shadows are shortest on any day. The east and the west are the points where the sun rises and sets at those times of the year when day and night are of equal length. Wherever we are, those cardinal points define our relationship to the wider cosmos and to the landscape in which we live. Bringing them down into the points of a circle is a natural and direct act which has little of the artificiality of setting up a compass in your living room to determine the four quarters.

In a very real sense, the magic circle is not just that line that we mark on the ground, but the great sphere of the heavens. When the night is dark and the stars are bright they sometimes feel close enough to touch - they are indeed part of our magic circle.

Indeed, this is the secret truth about astrology - our sphere, our aura, can expand to enclose the orbits of the planets. They are truly within us, are part of us and so we reflect their nature. From ancient times, people have responded to the Sun, Moon, planets and stars. People experienced them and their cycles directly and instinctively drew conclusions.

So our circle and sphere is within the circle and sphere of the heavens.

We may also be able to relate our circle to features in the surrounding landscape - perhaps hilltops, or bends in a river and, almost certainly, trees. The cardinal directions take on life and greater significance in an outdoor setting and perhaps other directions feature also.

The Wheel of the Year

A strong theme in Paganism is the yearly cycle and its reminder of the themes of life, death and rebirth.

The bare branches of the trees against the background of snow and mist, the new leaves gradually covering a whole tree with a bright green haze, the glory of the hawthorn blossom, the ripe grains of the field, scattered with bright red poppies against the deep rich greens of the oakwood, the variegated splendour of fallen leaves being swept into drifts by the biting cold wind - all show us the living nature of the place we have chosen. It is alive and shows different aspects of its character according to the season of the year.

We are thus far more aware of the cycle of the seasons if we celebrate outdoors. Our celebration will be also affected by the mood that the place itself is going through, in the same way that what we do and say is affected by the mood of someone we are close to.

What this means in practice is that, for example, the dates when we celebrate the seasonal festivals are determined not by some arbitrary calendar laid down in a book, but by what is actually happening in the landscape. If you are sensitive to, and observe, the living nature of the land, then you will know the right time to celebrate. It will, of course, vary from year to year, and it may be less convenient for planning your appointments diary, but you will find that this approach will put you much more in tune with the landscape than adherence to a strict timetable.

Also, the materials that we use and the actions we may partake in will, in some measure, be determined by the character of the site. Rituals held in the landscape have these themes strongly emphasised in their surroundings. The May Eve rite may be held surrounded by hawthorn trees in full flower. The Lammas ritual may be on the edge of a wheatfield waiting to be harvested. An autumn ritual may be held in a beech grove and the Candlemas ceremony may well be in a clearing in a wood that has snow still lying on the ground or on the tree branches. This makes the seasonal celebrations much more powerful and meaningful.

Just as certain sites suggest themselves as being at their best at certain times of the year so the site itself may suggest a particular way of celebrating. The varied colours of bramble leaves adjacent to one site may, for example, suggest a winter garland which used them, almost in the manner of a work of art by Andy Goldsworthy.

An autumn circle might indeed be formed by clearing the fallen leaves within a particular area, forming a ring around the outside which could subsequently be spread back over the circle to remove any traces. This could, of course, also be done in snow and, as an adaptation of the traditional "snowman", a representation of the Goddess might be sculpted in snow, being left, if possible, to melt back into the

Earth with the next thaw. The possibilities here are literally endless - the principle of responding spontaneously to the natural qualities inherent in the site and moment of time being the important thing.

Each year is therefore subtly, or even radically, different from the year before, and things certainly don't therefore become boring or predictable:

> *"The children always acted as if the Easter table was a surprise - although, of course, it was the same every year. The funny thing was, it always felt new and exciting."*[57]

The Moods of the Earth and Sky

There is little more changeable than the weather and it can rarely be fully appreciated indoors - its domain is the sky and the landscape. We must go out to meet it and, in the process, learn its lessons of constant change by using our senses to experience it.

One valuable clue is to flow with the varying quality of the weather and adapt what we do, rather than seeing it as a nuisance. We might emphasise in our ritual the elements that are prominent in the weather at the time. Thus, if it is very windy, we don't worry about how to keep the candles lit (those small glass lanterns you can get are very good, incidentally) but relax into the wind - let it take you over, become part of it, take the opportunity of getting to know it more intimately.

And there is nothing more exhilarating than performing a ritual skyclad in the rain if you can leave behind the everyday notion of worrying about things getting wet (a good waterproof bag and a towel are useful to have with you) and allow yourself to enjoy it, revel in it, feel part of the rain and of the earth which is soaking it up.

Words, Calls and Cries

One of the old witch traditions was that of calls and cries made at night in the remote countryside. The old witch calls were, in Patricia Crowther's words,

> "made with the intent of stimulating the spiritual and physical natures of the participants".[19]

As Gerald Gardner says:

> "In the good old days, when if you went half a mile from the village at night you could be sure no one would spy on you, because everyone not of the Craft was frightened to be out in the dark, it was possible to have the old dances, with plenty of music, to shrill out the calls, to have the chants and to make all the noise you wanted to"[32]

He goes on to say that the calls were long shrill cries which vibrate and produce terror. Perhaps in origin they started out as imitation of animal and bird cries, but there is a power in them which is both strange and awe-inspiring. The form of some of the cries has been written down but this conveys little of the real feeling behind it. From my own experience, I know that there is often an initial inhibition to full expression, but if that can be got through, then instinctive power takes over. The intellect takes a back seat and the effect is a magical one. Patricia Crowther gives the real feel of this:

> *"The essential purpose of calls is to stir the blood and make it quicken. For without these sonics, which literally thrill, any magical work will lack in potency.*
>
> *The ancient cries were always sent forth on the wind, from a hill top or other desolate meeting-place of the coven. The invoking calls were given by the leader before the commencement of the rites. They were, in the main, vowel sounds, which were the first sounds people made before learning how to use the lips and tongue for forming words. It has been found that with the use of these very primitive invocations, goose-pimples rise on the skin, and the hairs of one's head literally stand on end. This is evidence of a link between Divine Intelligence and the people concerned."*[19]

The reference to "sending forth on the wind" emphasises that this is an outdoor activity. What seems to be happening is that energy is being built up, which is, through the physical form of echoes, returned to create that link between the individual or group and their surroundings. It is perhaps the same sort of thing that bats do.

Sounds have power and they have meaning. These have been kept secret because of this and are only uttered in very special circumstances. Words are a development of this. Names have power and this is the reason for God and Goddess names being kept secret. The uttering of a secret name in the right circumstances can be a very powerful thing, partly for this reason. Often secret names can come to us at such times.

Witches have traditions of an old half-forgotten language, possibly connected to the Basque, the oldest known language in Europe. Such words may be known to that hidden part of ourselves and can cause a powerful echo to reverberate in our being, due to their deep associations.

CHAPTER 11

EMBRACING THE SITE

Movement is natural to all living beings, even plants following the daily course of the sun. Whilst there is a place for stilling the body and mind in 'sitting out', walking meditation, where we are very slowly moving in response to our environment, is a valid action. As a response to the joy of being at one with Nature, movement is instinctive. Dancing, and particularly circle dancing, is one of the earliest of such responses, and images of this have been found in cave paintings dating from Palaeolithic times.

It helps to approach such dancing clothed in the right way. For me, this means going skyclad, i.e. naked, about which Doreen Valiente has this to say:

> *"Ritual nudity as a magical practice is very old. The naked dances organized by the pagan cult of witchcraft in times past were denounced by the Church; but they still took place. In those days, when the countryside was much more thinly populated than it is today, large bonfires could be lit in lonely places, to provide light and warmth, and a gay glowing centre of magic flame to dance around. By dancing naked, in a state of mind of 'oneness with nature', witches contacted the universal life energy, and felt themselves revitalized."*[83]

I am aware that some witchcraft traditions did not practice nudity. Equally certainly, however, some did. A careful reading of Gerald Gardner's books, for example, reveals that the New Forest witches with whom he first made contact in 1938 practiced ritual nudity. And Leland, in *"Aradia, or the Gospel of the Witches"* (1890), makes it quite clear that nakedness was a central part of their rites: "And as the sign that ye are truly free, ye shall be naked in your rites..."[47]

It is often said that, because witches traditionally met out of doors, ritual nudity would have been impractical in England because of our climate. There are several reasons why this is not necessarily so. Our climate is actually warm enough to allow going skyclad for quite a bit of the year. The old country people were more hardy than we largely are today with our centrally heated houses and offices. They spent much of their time out of doors and had become used to rather lower temperatures. It is actually quite extraordinary, but I have often noted how one does not feel that much colder in the nude than when fully dressed. Traditionally, the witches certainly used to have dark robes and walk to their meeting place. This would not only discourage detection, but robes would be easy to discard and put back on. It is easy to perform part of a ritual skyclad and then put on a robe for the more sedentary part of the proceedings, such as the feast.

It is also the tradition that goose fat was rubbed on the skin, with certain hallucinatory and other ingredients added. This would only be possible and effective if clothes had been first removed. Some of the ingredients may themselves have contributed to keeping out the cold or allowing the individual to withstand it more easily, as Gerald Gardner says:

"... I have been shown a recipe for an anointing oil. This consisted of vervain, or mint crushed and steeped in olive oil or lard, left overnight, then squeezed through a

cloth to remove the leaves. Fresh leaves were then added and the squeezing repeated three or four times until it was strongly scented and ready for use. It is said that if they lived in the country where they would not be seen, they would strip and rub the oil into their skin and go to the sabbat naked. This would keep them warm enough until they reached the dance."[32]

Besides the more magical functions of circle dancing, the other, practical, purpose, was to keep warm. The traditional central fire clearly performed a similar function.

Whilst there are limits, one of the functions of the seasonal rituals is to bring us into contact with the "spirit of the season" - for certain festivals, this would include feeling the cold air. Shamanic or trance states could be induced which inured those participating to feeling the cold, as has been chronicled in various parts of the world.

For many years, I have felt that there were many benefits to be derived from going skyclad during rituals. Many of these have been put forward before, but it may be useful to set them out again:

One is demonstrating that the particular time and space where the ritual is being performed is something special, set aside from everyday life.

One is more in tune with and closer to nature, experiencing not just the wind on one's body, but also the thorns, stinging nettles, hard twigs and stones on one's feet!

If you are performing the ritual with others, there is a definite feeling of letting down barriers, of which clothes are symbolic. As a result, we can draw closer together. It is often said that bodies, particularly of those past the first flush of youth, are ugly. This is the sort of thinking, where we compare ourselves to some artificial ideal created by the advertising agents, fashion houses and film producers, that I hope we can get away from and learn to accept each other as we are. We have the image of the triple Goddess before us: Maiden, Mother and Crone are equally part of life, and so are their male equivalents.

There is something so powerful and liberating when I take off my clothes prior to a ritual that any intellectual arguments to the contrary can have little effect. I am not asking anyone to change the way they do things, but if they have not gone to some remote spot and removed their clothes at midnight under a full moon as an act of worship of the Goddess, then I would suggest that they might be missing something. I don't want to over-emphasise this, as it is far better to wear robes or even ordinary clothes to meet the Goddess than to stay away.

Dancing has a physical, emotional and spiritual effect on us and may have an effect on the Earth as well and it has been said that the Earth likes to be touched, to be massaged by our dancing feet. If there are aromatic herbs growing then there will be wafts of the scent as your feet stir them as you dance.

Trevor James Constable and others have confirmed that there are beings living in the atmosphere whose images can be caught on infra-red film. He attracts them by means of what he calls The Star Exercise, a sort of slow dance.[17] Andrew Collins and others have recently successfully repeated this.[16]

Traditionally, witches have justified the circle dance as a means of raising the Cone of Power. As Doreen Valiente says:

"... when a circle of naked or loosely robed dancers gyrates in a witchcraft ceremony, the power flowing from their bodies rises upwards towards the centre of the circle, forming a cone-shape which is called the Cone of Power. This is directable by the concentrated will of those present to carry out the object of the ceremony, by bearing its influence from the physical to the more subtle planes of the universe, where the power of will and imagination can, in turn, affect the physical again and influence material events."[84]

The participants hold hands and walk and run round the circle deosil (i.e. sun-wise or clockwise) as fast as they can, often chanting some phrase or rhyme and concentrating intensely on the objective behind the ritual.

I mentioned in Chapter 8 the effect which dancing or running the maze has on the state of mind of the participants and, in a sense, Constable's Star Exercise, the rhythmic threading of the maze and the circle dance to raise the cone of power are all forms of the same basic activity - raising power through purposeful patterned movement. Just as Constable could attract entities living in the atmosphere, so any form of ritual held in the countryside will attract the attention of nature spirits in the vicinity, as I describe elsewhere.

We need to be reminded, however, that dancing is not essential, particularly as there are many who, by reason of such things as physical disability, cannot participate in that way. Alastair Clay-Egerton puts it into context:

"So you can't spin like a Whirling Dervish, one of the Sufi who are so rightly known as the "Witches of Islam". Don't worry about it. Not all the Sufis are "Turners" or Whirl about until they reach a state of trance or semi-

175

trance. Many Sufi stand or sit quite still and use their minds. The Moon no longer rotates, but it still has a powerful gravitational field. Those of us who can not join in the ring dances can still create, by our minds and will, revolving circles which, despite not being on the physical plane may still be powerful.

In fact, being mental creations they may be more powerful than those created with such physical effort in the physical plane by our swift, sure-footed and sweaty able-bodied colleagues. So fear not! What the disabled witch may lack in physical abilities they may well make up for in mental or spiritual achievement. The disabled Witch may well be able to sing "I could have danced all night," and add, "but I preferred to save my physical energy and use my mind instead!"[12]

Dancing is only one of the significant physical actions which may be performed. Embracing the Earth can literally mean just this - lying full-length on the ground, face down, feeling the earth, including the stones, bumps in the ground, and plants, with your whole body. The other senses, particularly of scent and sound, will of course also come into play.

Alternatively, we can lie on our back, looking up at the stars through the trees. The link with the infinity of space at the same time as we are supported by and in contact with the Earth can be an immensely moving experience.

Dancing and purposeful movement of the body can have a very definite effect on others who are watching. This is a language that is deeper than words and its motivation comes from an area that is deeper than thought. If we can tune in sufficiently to the place and to each other then things can be expressed that are totally spontaneous, totally beyond words and yet totally meaningful. And there are also certain secret gestures that are powerful because they communicate directly with the deepest part of our being.

In any discussion of significant physical actions, sex must have a central role, and it may be useful to ask what sex is about.

One answer is that it is about excitement, a contrast from the usual state of being; it is about personal involvement in what is happening, often intense personal involvement; and it is a focus, a peak experience in the midst of the happenings of everyday life.

I must emphasise that I am not just including sexual experience with a partner nor am I limiting it to a particular sexual orientation. In my own experience, and I would imagine that I am not alone, sex involves a gradual or even fairly sudden build-up of excitement to the point of orgasm followed by a state of relaxation, often intense relaxation, when I can let go of all tensions and feel energy flowing through me.

One of the special things about sex is that, at the moment of orgasm, we are truly in the present, even if only momentarily - a focal point showing our whole being what is potentially possible.

Sometimes, and this usually happens when I am alone in some remote wild place, perhaps a wood or beside a waterfall, spring or rock outcrop, I experience what can only be described as strong sexual feelings. They are not directed towards another person, nor do I have fantasies about anyone else being there. The feelings seem to be directed towards my surroundings and the energies that underlie the landscape.

Sex is one of the eight ways of magic and is therefore one of the ways of raising power for magical purposes. It is, however, also something just to be enjoyed, and where better than in the open air. Guy Ragland Phillips says:

> *"It is essential that a natural function should be carried out in as natural a manner and in as natural conditions as possible. Copulation in bed is all very well, but it is a very pale imitation compared with coupling naked in the sunshine on top of a mountain. It is not only that the lovers are missing something if they confine their love to a darkened bedroom instead of the embrace of nature; it is also that they are robbing nature of something that belongs to her, for love is nothing if it is not sacramental and should be offered to nature (by whatever name you give her). It is true that the sun does not always shine, even on lovers, and on mountain tops the wind can be cool enough to quench the strongest ardour. Never mind - there are other delectable places. Chances on the mountains, on the lonely beach or in the forest should never be missed, for there you touch not only each other but nature herself at the same time, full length and all around. Those who have done it know this is proper: what might perhaps be termed a Whole Earth Offering or Whole Earth Communion"*[64]

The places that lovers choose to make love are very often the sort of places we have been talking about - beautiful locations a little bit out of the way. I saw some beautiful love nests once close to a hawthorn hedge in a field of wheat about to be harvested - they were smaller and a more organic shape than corn circles. It would be interesting to see whether, by sympathetic magic, the yields from that field were higher the following year.

Of course, the vegetation is sometimes uncomfortable, and at certain seasons there are flies to contend with, but there is something so archetypally right about making love in the open air that these are moments that are remembered in a very special way.

The Use of Working Tools

I do not wish to add to the profusion of words which have been written on ritual tools and I will therefore limit myself to taking just three examples, the altar, the wand and the garland, looking at the way we interact with the site and how magical tools can emerge from the place itself.

This has echoes of very ancient practice indeed. In some traditions, metal, particularly iron, is not allowed inside the circle. I have always thought that this may have been a faint echo or memory brought through from Neolithic times, seeing metal as associated with the invaders - modern and not appropriate for the old Craft, as today most pagans might be reluctant to use plastic in the circle. It might also be that metal was not found naturally within the area and was therefore foreign in nature. Where metal was admitted, as knives, for example, they merely had a practical use for cutting rather than any more esoteric function.

I want to look at magical tools which can be found in or adapted from the site itself, emphasising that link with the land. At the deepest level, the only working tools we need are our own body, mind and spirit and if we are in tune with the land we will need nothing else. Artifacts can be powerful symbols, however, and can be a valuable help to us by acting as a focus for our conscious mind.

A hawthorn tree of distinctive shape which acts as an altar in a ritual circle.

There are several principles associated with the making and using of magical tools which may be worth exploring in order to get a general "feel" for them.

They appear when the time is right, either as a gift to us or as something so obvious we can't miss it.

We should make or fashion them ourselves, putting ourselves into them with each action that we take, impregnating them with our vibrations, as it were.

They should only be shown to or handled by very few others.

The two apparently conflicting, but ultimately resolvable, sides of the same principle - one that tools should only be used for magical purposes, the other that they should be everyday items that become closely associated with you by regular use.

Working tools should, as far as possible, be obtained locally to where you are going to be using them as there is a certain power in taking to a site ritual tools as many as possible of which came from there in the first place or are of materials which can be found there.

There will be a spot which is the point on which the site is focused, perhaps several spots, perhaps just one. There will be somewhere which you will become aware of as the centre, probably not the physical centre, but somewhere which seems to embody the spirit of the place. This is the spot which is right for your altar. It could well be a tree or a rock or perhaps just a patch of ground. I have known an altar which was a fork in a tree trunk forming a natural bowl which held rain water. Fallen tree trunks often provide somewhere suitable and I have also known of an altar built up from sticks found lying on the woodland floor, before being covered with an altar cloth.

A natural-occurring altar may not coincide with our preconceived ideas of locating it in the north, east or wherever. Perhaps in this case, it is we who have to change to accommodate the site. If we are not used to having the altar in the south-west, for example, perhaps using it there will teach us something we wouldn't otherwise know. What emerges may not be an altar in the conventional sense - a raised flat area for putting things on - but it is always appropriate - we adapt to it, rather than the other way round. The important thing is to feel what is right in the particular location and flow with that.

The wand, traditionally cut from hazel, (though other woods can be used, each conveying its own distinctive character) is probably the most basic and primitive magical tool - certainly more ancient than the knife or athame. It is for directing energy and concentrating power.

The way I acquired my own wand is interesting. I had been wanting a wand, but the time hadn't seemed right. I had been told that, according to a particular tradition, wands can only be cut at a certain time of day on only two specific days in the year.

Some time later, I was driving to a conference at the other end of the country. I wanted a rest and drove off the motorway, and found a quiet lane. I took a short walk and, not far from where I had parked the car, I found myself looking at a magnificent hazel tree. I began to think that there were some good branches there suitable for a wand and that it was a pity I was not there in the two moments in the year that wands could be cut. It took me some time before I realised that, in fact, it was actually within minutes of being one of the key moments in the year.

As the realisation spread in me, I had this overwhelming feeling that this was meant to be and that I could cut my wand. I did so - it came away easily. I gave thanks to the tree. The wand has been a most powerful tool and is still growing in power.

Whether you keep it in its natural state or remove the bark, smooth and polish it thoroughly probably depends on your inclination. I keep mine in its natural state with very little additional work. I do keep it wrapped up and it only sees the light of day (or moonlight more often) when I am actually using it. One tradition is that it should be kept wrapped and buried in the ground when not in use. This may be to maintain its charge of Earth power, or a practical precaution during times of persecution.

One of the most powerful tools, albeit by its nature a temporary one, is the garland. This is made up of seasonal flowers, leaves, fruits, grain etc. I usually make one in a ring, of a suitable size to use as a head-dress, made from any flexible plant stem such as clematis, honeysuckle, Russian vine, etc. Form it into a circle with green garden twine (not the plastic kind) and add the seasonal flowers etc. with more twine. This holds them tightly. To keep the garland fresh until needed, spray it with water and keep it in a plastic bag. In some traditions, the garland is placed on the stang or the altar. It can be worn during the celebrations and can then be offered to a tree in the vicinity, where it will decay naturally over the coming weeks.

Many other working tools, such as the stang (a walking stick which is a disguise for its true function as a portable altar. It is usually ash and the same principles apply to its acquisition as apply to the wand) and the necklace, can be made with materials from your ritual site. I have made a necklace by going about on hands and knees at midnight during the Dark of the Moon in an old oak grove, collecting acorns which are then sorted, drilled and threaded.

Giving and Taking

The whole universe flows and is a continuous round of giving and receiving, each action necessary to ensure that its living nature is maintained. We are part of that universe and what we are doing is valid and right. We do not need to offer gifts if we are fully centred. If something needs to be done it will occur naturally - it should not be forced or artificial.

But it is so natural, in my experience, to offer flowers, for example, at a ritual that it seems to be something archetypal and right, not because we see ourselves as separate from nature and have to make offerings but because we are part of it and by our action can bring certain things together that were previously separate, such as laying flowers on a tree altar.

If you keep your eyes open and know likely places to look, you will quite frequently see offerings that people have made, usually a small bunch of flowers, leaves, grasses or berries, gathered nearby. They may be lodged in some crevice in a rock, floated in a pool or simply laid at the base of a tree trunk. They can easily be missed but are an indication that someone cares for the spirit of the place.

It is in their nature, being gathered locally, that offerings of this kind will be seasonal in character. Normally, if they are left, they will disappear from view in a fairly short time and not be noticeable to the casual passer-by.

Occasionally, some other offering might feel right. I have seen a very beautiful goddess harvest loaf which was left under a tree and doubtless consumed by woodland creatures within a short time. I would be reluctant to leave anything of a permanent nature, such as crystals or stones, for reasons given earlier and because in a sense it might be seen as polluting the site.

There is, however, a tradition of burying ears of wheat, barley and oats at the autumn equinox - they will come through as green shoots in the winter and spring, with the hope of being harvested the following Lammas. This can continue over several years and is a living reminder of the cycles of life, death and rebirth of which we are a part.

This approach of things being natural and right can also be adopted when you feel that you need to take something from the site. Nature is bounteous and if it is right that you should have something then she will give unstintingly. The example I gave of finding my wand is, I think, typical of the feeling which one gets. Things seem to fall right if you really need the item in question and have an open approach that recognises something when you see it. Clearly, there are quite a few things involved here including being clear why you want something, even if it is an inner conviction without an obvious present need.

The procedure to adopt may be an elaborate tradition, based on particular times for doing things, or it may arise from a sensitivity to the needs of plants and trees and avoiding any unnecessary harm. Part of this is certainly asking the tree or plant for permission for what you want to do, explaining the reasons in an ordinary straightforward way, and taking heed of any answer we get. Even if we do not feel that we are sensitive enough to experience the response, we are assured that there is a response and that, if we are willing, we will know whether it is right to proceed.

Acting Spontaneously

Probably one of the main points of difference between pagan groups is the extent to which their rituals are planned in advance. At one extreme, everyone has a text and their own part to perform, which they read in turn until the last page.

It is very much like amateur dramatics. At its best, I am sure such ceremonies can be meaningful and moving, but in my experience the emphasis is too often on the amateur. Lines are forgotten (I am certainly not innocent of this myself!), your place in the script is lost and, having put down the paper at some critical point in the ritual, it proceeds to blow away! Gathering gloom after sunset means that the latter pages are unreadable, and so on ...

I know I exaggerate somewhat, but it seems to me that if you are calling on the Goddess to inspire you then you have to be prepared to allow that to happen.

I advocate a Quaker form of paganism and to explain this I really need to say a little bit about the Quakers. They started in the wilds of Westmorland in the 17th Century, rejecting all outward forms, and seeing the whole of life as sacramental. The Quaker meetings are held in silence until someone is moved by the spirit to speak. In the terms used by Joseph Campbell, Quakerism is on the wing of Christianity closest to the Type I religions.

It is said that, at the worst time of persecution of the witches, Quakers were one of the few who would help them.

In more recent years, that writer on paganism, Guy Ragland Phillips, helped to found the Universalist tradition, which supported the widening of the specifically Christian mode of expression within Quakerism to encompass other faiths, including paganism.

So, when I talk about a Quaker form of paganism, I mean one which is spontaneous, waits upon the spirit and rejects outer forms.

In many ways, traditional witchcraft is similar to this. Despite the controversial writings of W.E. Liddell ('Lugh')[49], much traditional witchcraft is lost in a mist of uncertainty, ambiguity and speculation. However, it is certainly true that much of what I have written in this book is in sympathy with such traditions.

For example, it is almost certain that they never had set rituals that were written down, and this is the true reason why Gerald Gardner invented so much - the New Forest witches had no written rituals and set ways of doing things to write about. Their workings, in common with those in other parts of the country, were largely spontaneous, tailored to the specific matter in hand. So we need not be surprised that Gardner felt he had not just to 'fill in the gaps' but virtually start from scratch when it came to writing something down.

It is very much a question of direction. Do you want to direct the ritual or do you want to put yourself in the hands of the Goddess? Whilst a set form of words can be limiting to a ritual, words themselves can be immensely powerful.

The answer to this apparent dilemma may lie in having a stock of short and powerful things which can be said if appropriate, coupled with spontaneous utterances. In fact, many of the most moving rituals I have taken part in have been largely silent.

Practical Considerations

Most of the practicalities are really fairly obvious.

Many rituals take place at night, so make sure you can find your way there. If you have followed the advice in this book, you will have visited the site a few times to get to know it in any case. However, places look very different by the light of the Moon: on a dark cloudy night it may be very difficult indeed. Even if your ritual is at sunset it can be very dark when you have finished and you may well have to rely on all your senses to find your way out.

Even if it is a site you have used several times previously, it is as well to visit a day or so before to make sure everything is all right and to prepare the place if necessary.

Even with the spontaneous, flowing rituals I have been advocating, it is surprising how many things you may want to take. The following list is an example (in no particular order): candles, glasses to put candles in, matches, incense, bowl for incense, charcoal blocks, sand to put in bowl, water, cakes and wine, athame, wand, stang, garland, altar cloth, torch ...

I am sure I have missed something! Don't forget the matches - or the torch! You may have the very best of intentions about leaving the site as you found it, but it is very easy to leave something behind in the dark, and the torch is very useful.

A good rucksack is probably the best thing for carrying everything in, particularly if you have to walk any distance.

Feeling the Response

Our own actions may be little more than pump-priming. The wisdom of the Goddess, the joy that we can sense in experiencing her living being - the Spirit in the Earth - is on occasions so overwhelming, such a generous response, that we are swept up with the joy of the experience - that sense of connectedness and of being part of some wider whole.

I have experienced this response as impersonal but welcoming, have been strongly aware of a presence and have seen that presence in misty forms gathering around the circle. It is the sort of experience that can really only be referred to obliquely - in a poetic sort of way - so I will finish by quoting what others have felt. Firstly, Evan John Jones:

> "... on some occasions the symbol becomes reality. The wine and cakes are charged with the power of the Goddess. When this occurs, a subtle change comes over the rites. Instead of you working the rites, the ritual starts working you. From the moment the knife touches the wine, everything the group intends doing goes by the board. Instinctively everyone knows what to do next and what is to follow. It is very similar to the action of the spark plugs of an engine - bang, bang, bang, and the power flows! The union between the Goddess and the congregation is a two-way flow of energy or force, set in an area of non-time. Everything in the circle seems to stand still for this period. There is a feeling of heightened awareness and emotion. Things are felt with a greater intensity and understanding. Somehow, for a few moments, time and place cease to exist. You then know what it means to be able to spin without motion between two worlds.
>
> Even though everyone feels physically drained by this, a sense of euphoria seems to well up from deep inside. Every one of the senses seems to be in some way enhanced. Things take on a clarity and intensity that are not of this world. Knowledge and instinct become intertwined and as one. Everybody knows with certainty that they have seen and felt some part of the magic of the circle."[43]

Whilst I imagine Michael Bentine would not describe himself as pagan, he gives a very vivid account of an experience which comes within that broad definition of paganism with which I started this book:

"The night was calm and quite warm, with a few lazy clouds drifting across the moonlit sky. We walked silently in single file through the lush ferns that now rustled round us. The dense underbrush continued as we passed into the thick clumps of trees which made up the small wood. Here the light was considerably reduced, yet Eddie continued to lead the way effortlessly.

Quite unexpectedly, we came out of the clusters of saplings and mature trees into a small clearing, which must have been centrally placed in the wood, and there Eddie stopped. The moon had come out from behind a large billowing cloud and now lit the whole scene almost as brightly as daylight, but with a soft silvery light. You could almost hear the silence.

Eddie turned to me as I stood a few feet behind him just in front of my father. He smiled, and gestured to me to listen. Then he turned and, in a low voice, halfway between a whistle and a word, gave one strange, short gentle call.

Immediately, from every corner of the wood, the birds, the beasts, even the insects and, I felt, every tree and plant, answered him!

It was a great, joyous, chorus of greeting to a much loved friend.

There was no 'alarm' in that spontaneous answer - just a massive response of nature to nature: like attracting like.

Tears streamed down my face and I could see my father crying too - marvellous natural tears of joy that seemed to wash away the fears and doubts that had assailed me, reaffirming that nature is far stronger than man alone. I shall never forget that moment!"[3]

ENDWORDS

Attempting any conclusion or trying to draw a few threads together is rather difficult because what I have sought to do in writing this book is to open up the range of possibilities and to suggest particular directions which might be fruitful to follow. I have had the lofty aim of providing inspiration, like the picture on the seed packet, showing what might be attainable.

One thing that it is important to remember is that paganism is not an organisation but a movement. Nobody is in a position of power within a hierarchy telling you what to do. This is certainly liberating but it does put the responsibility firmly on you to decide what you are going to do and where you are going to do it. You have a contribution to make and that contribution will help to determine how paganism will be seen in the future.

Paganism is, at its root, about our relationship with the Earth, and thus with the Earth Goddess. I have suggested that this can more easily and naturally be accomplished in her own special realm - the landscape itself - and I hope I have opened a door towards that, or at any rate given hints as to where a key might be found.

In any relationship we have to listen, and that means being sensitive and adaptable, leaving behind our preconceived ideas and allowing ourselves to be moved by the spirit.

I hope I have encouraged you to make the effort to go out and get to know those secret places of the Goddess. If you can find that sensitivity within yourself, you will be guided towards the place that is right for you and will be open enough to respond spontaneously to the Spirit of Place that you find there.

Whilst it is difficult for me to put into words, one of the feelings which quite often comes over me when I am participating in a ritual at a special place in the landscape is that I am not alone.

By this I mean not only the animals and spirits of the place that are attracted by what is going on, and the sometimes strong presence of what Evan John Jones calls the "Hidden Company" - witches and pagans from years gone by who frequented the place and watch over us. No, I am also strongly aware of everyone else who, at that moment, is standing under a tree meditating, sitting writing poetry, making love beside the running stream or performing a ritual in a forest clearing. There is such a strong feeling of connection, of companionship in what we all in our diverse ways are doing, that is so comforting and supportive.

My hope is that this book will in some small way have encouraged the growth of that companionship and support.

FURTHER READING

I haven't found many books which devote much space to special places in the landscape, and this is really the reason why I decided to write this book.

There are certainly scattered pieces in several books and assorted articles, many of which I quote and details of which will be found in the "References" section.

However, I must mention the books of Marian Green and Doreen Valiente. I have long admired these, and there is much that is wise and inspiring amongst their pages. Above all, they are both very readable authors!

For consistency and quality, the magazine "The Cauldron" (subtitled "Pagan Journal of the Old Religion"), obtainable from Mike Howard, Caemorgan Cottage, Caemorgan Road, Cardigan, Dyfed SA43 1QU (DO NOT PUT "THE CAULDRON" ON THE ENVELOPE) is one of the best; and The Pagan Federation, BM Box 7097, London WC1N 3XX is a good organisation to join if you want to keep in touch with what is happening in the pagan movement and make contact with local groups.

The real message of this book, however, is that "further reading" is really far less important than further exploration and experience of those special places in the landscape. They can teach you far more than any books ever can.

REFERENCES

1. Appleton, Jay The Experience of Landscape (Wiley 1975)
2. Barry Ye ex Pedant Finding Your Way in the Woods (Berkana 1991)
3. Bentine, Michael The Door Marked Summer (Granada 1981)
4. Beth, Rae Hedge Witch (Hale 1990)
5. Blacker, Carmen The Catalpa Bow (Unwin 1986)
6. Bucke, Richard M. Cosmic Consciousness (Dutton 1901)
7. Campanelli, Dan and Pauline Circles Groves and Sanctuaries (Llewellyn 1993)
8. Campbell, Joseph The Masks of God (4 volumes) (Viking Penguin 1959-68)
9. Capra, Fritjof The Tao of Physics (Wildwood House 1975)
10. Cartwright, Julia The Pilgrim's Way (J. S. Virtue & Co. 1895)
11. Castaneda, Carlos The Teachings of Don Juan (University of California Press 1968)
12. Clay-Egerton, Alastair 'Non-Rotary' in Cheiron News Oimelc 1992 Vol 1 No 2
13. Clay-Egerton, Mériém (unpublished manuscript)
14. Cochrane, Robert 'The Witches' Esbat', in The Cauldron 63 Winter 1992
15. Collins, Andrew The Seventh Sword (Century 1991)
16. Collins, Andrew Alien Energy (ABC Books 1994)
17. Constable, Trevor James The Cosmic Pulse of Life (Merlin Press 1976)
18. Crowley, Vivianne Wicca (Aquarian 1989)
19. Crowther, Patricia Lid Off the Cauldron (Muller 1981)
20. Cunningham Scott Magical Aromatherapy (Llewellyn 1989)
21. Devereux, Paul Earth Memory (Quantum 1991)
22. Dickinson, Bob 'Kirton Lindsey Holy Wells' in Markstone 3 Summer 1990
23. Dickinson, Bob 'Lud's Well, Stainton-le-Vale' in Markstone 3 Summer 1990
24. Dickinson, Bob 'The Holy Unspeakable Name' in Markstone 6 Spring 1992

25	Edhel 'The Pool' in Touchwood Vol 2 No 5 Beltaine 1989
26	Ellis, Robin 'The Woods Between the Worlds' in The Deosil Dance 34 Imbolc 1993
27	Farrar, Janet and Stewart Eight Sabbats for Witches (Hale 1981)
28	Fortune, Dion The Goat-Foot God (William and Norgate 1936)
29	Fortune, Dion The Sea Priestess (1938, republished Aquarian 1957)
30	Frazer, James D. The Golden Bough (Macmillan 1922)
31	Gardner, Gerald B. (Scire) High Magic's Aid (Michael Houghton 1949)
32	Gardner, Gerald B. Witchcraft Today (Rider 1954)
33	Gibran, Kahlil The Prophet (Heinemann 1923)
34	Golding, Laurence 'Holywell at Sunset' in Wood and Water Vol 2 No 3 Beltane 1982
35	Graves, Robert The White Goddess (Faber and Faber 1952)
36	Green, Marian The Elements of Natural Magic (Element Books 1989)
37	Green, Marian A Witch Alone (Aquarian 1991)
38	Harte, Jeremy 'Haunted Roads' in The Ley Hunter 121 Summer 1994
39	Heselton, Philip (with Jimmy Goddard and Paul Baines) Skyways and Landmarks Revisited, (Northern Earth Mysteries Group/Surrey Earth Mysteries Group 1985)
40	Hiley, Denise 'Impressions of Nature' in New Dimensions September 1991
41	Hopkins, R. Thurston Sussex Pilgrimages (1927)
42	Jackson, Nigel Aldcroft The Call of the Horned Piper (Capall Bann 1994)
43	Jones, Evan John (with Doreen Valiente) Witchcraft - A Tradition Renewed (Hale 1990)
44	Kent, Elizabeth Picnic Basket (Fontana 1978)
45	Koppana Kati-Ma Forest Spirits (Mandragora Dimensions 1992)
46	Langstone, Alex 'The White Lady' in The Lighthouse 1 Vernal Equinox 1993
47	Leland, Charles Godfrey Aradia: or the Gospel of the Witches (David Nutt 1899)
48	Lethbridge, T.C. The Essential T.C. Lethbridge, ed. Tom Graves and Janet Hoult, (Routledge and Kegan Paul 1980)
49	Liddell, W.E. The Pickingill Papers (Capall Bann 1994)
50	Mabey, Richard The Unofficial Countryside (Collins 1973)

51 Mason, Stanley Weston Kestrels over the Beacon (Brockhampton Press 1949)
52 Matthews, John 'Breaking the Circle' in Voices from the Circle ed. Prudence Jones and Caitlin Matthews, (Aquarian 1990)
53 Michell, John The Earth Spirit (Thames and Hudson 1975)
54 Michell, John Simulacra (Thames and Hudson 1979)
55 Milne, A.A. The House at Pooh Corner (Methuen 1928)
56 Mirov N.T. and Hasbrouck, J. The Story of Pines (Indiana University Press 1976)
57 Mooney, Bel I Know! (Methuen 1991)
58 Morris, William 'Under an Elm Tree' in Political Writings of William Morris ed. A.L. Morton (Lawrence and Wishart 1973)
59 Murray, Margaret A. The Witch-Cult in Western Europe (Oxford University Press 1921)
60 Nicholson, John Folk-Lore of East Yorkshire (Simpkin Marshall 1890)
61 Padfield, Tony 'To Fetch Thee Home' in Wood and Water 3 Winter 1979-80
62 Pennick, Nigel Practical Magic in the Northern Tradition (Aquarian 1989)
63 Pennick, Nigel Anima Loci (Nideck 1993)
64 Phillips, Guy Ragland '... Gets in Touch' in Wood and Water 4 Spring 1980
65 Ramsay, Hartley Edward Elgar (undated)
66 Ransome, Arthur Swallowdale (Jonathan Cape 1931)
67 Raven, Morgan 'Communicating with Nature Spirits' in The Unicorn 4
68 Richardson, Alan Priestess (Aquarian 1987)
69 Richardson, Janian 'Southstone, near Stanford Bridge, Worcestershire' in Wood and Water 7 Halloween 1980
70 Rider, Carl Your Psychic Power and How to Develop It (Piatkus 1988)
71 Rudkin, Ethel H. Lincolnshire Folklore (Beltons 1936)
72 Ryall, Rhiannon West Country Wicca (1989, republished Capall Bann 1993)
73 Selene 'Spiritual 'Re-charge' in a Welsh Wood' in Balefire Vol 5 No 7 Spring Equinox 1983
74 Sheldrake, Rupert A New Science of Life (Blond and Briggs 1981)
75 Simons, Paul 'Sounds the hills are alive with' in The Guardian 6 October 1994
76 Symes, Keith 'Goddess Temples' in The Cauldron 14 May Eve 1979

77	Taplin, Kim The English Path (Boydell Press 1979)
78	Taplin, Kim Tongues in Trees (Green Books 1989)
79	Taylor, Ian The All Saints' Ley Hunt (Northern Lights 1986)
80	Thomas, Anna The Vegetarian Epicure (Vintage Books 1972)
81	Valiente, Doreen Where Witchcraft Lives (Aquarian 1962)
82	Valiente, Doreen An ABC of Witchcraft Past and Present (Hale 1973)
83	Valiente, Doreen Natural Magic (Hale 1975)
84	Valiente, Doreen Witchcraft for Tomorrow (Hale 1978)
85	Valiente, Doreen The Rebirth of Witchcraft (Hale 1989)
86	Ward, Colin Anarchy in Action (George Allen and Unwin 1973)
87	Watkins, Allen 'The Straight Path in Wisdom Teaching' in The Ley Hunter 18 1971
88	Wedd, Tony 'The Way, The Truth and the Light' in The Ley Hunter 3 January 1970
89	Wedd, Tony T for Tomorrow (unpublished manuscript)
90	Whelan, Edna and Taylor, Ian Yorkshire Holy Wells and Sacred Springs (Northern Lights 1989)
91	Wilks, J.H. Trees of the British Isles in History and Legend (Muller 1972)
92	Wilson, Stephanie 'Out of the Silent Rock' in Wood and Water Vol 2 No 30 Winter Solstice 1989

INDEX

Access, 50, 89, 110, 115, 128
acorns, 183
Air, 25, 29, 33, 37, 57, 60, 69, 71, 79, 95, 135, 137-140, 164, 173, 178-179
alchemists, 21, 137
alder, 94
altars, 179-184, 188
altered states of consciousness, 143, 146-147
American tradition, 5
anarchism, 7
Anima Loci, 13, 196
animal tracks, 87
anointing oil, 172
aromatherapy, 136, 194
aromatic herbs, 136-137, 174
art, 26, 161, 166
ash, 3, 10, 32, 37-38, 68, 89, 183
Ashdown Forest, 40, 88
astral projection, 88, 90
astrology, 73, 75, 109, 144, 165
athame, 182, 188
aura, 9, 20, 26, 33, 48, 53, 56, 62, 109-110, 146, 165
Australian natives, 5, 121
Autumn, 10, 16, 47, 166, 185

Bach, Edward, 77
badger paths, 87
Baines, Paul, 29, 137, 195
beacons, 85, 196
beech, 4, 6, 12, 32, 37-42, 45-49, 94, 118, 124, 126, 129, 157, 166
Beltane, 118, 195
Bentine, Michael, 53, 189, 194

Beth, Rae, 89, 194
Beth-Luis-Nion, 40
birch, 10, 37-38, 62, 71, 94-95, 118
bird song, 142, 147
birds, 3, 116, 132, 144, 151, 155, 163, 190
birdseed, 160, 163
Blacker, Carmen, 16, 194
bleeding yew, 124
blossom, 37, 138, 155, 165
bonfires, 82, 142137, 171
Boundaries, 4, 33, 35, 37, 49-51, 80, 98, 111, 118, 129, 133, 135, 144-145
Box, 38, 73, 97, 193
brambles, 25, 108, 122, 133, 157
briars, 62, 152
Bucke, R. M., 14-15, 194
Buddhism, 11
burial chambers, 23

cakes, 188-189
Calls, 37, 42, 97, 110, 124, 168-169, 174, 192
Campbell, Joseph, 11, 14, 186, 194
Cancer, 75
Candlemas, 118, 166
candles, 167, 188
Capra, Fritjof, 14-15, 194
cardinal points, 162-164
Cartwright, Julia, 73, 194
Castaneda, Carlos, 96, 194
cattle tracks, 74
Cauldron, 193-194, 196
caves, 24-25, 55-56, 62, 68, 81, 89, 171

cave paintings, 55, 171
cedar, 83, 138
ch'i, 21
chakras, 109, 146
chalk, 25, 53, 57, 59-60, 74, 89, 126, 128
chalk pits, 57, 59
Chanctonbury Ring, 42-43
chants, 168
children, 7, 135, 167
churches, 10, 56, 95
churchyards, 30, 124
circles, 10, 38, 42, 45, 50-51, 75-76, 83, 88, 91, 129, 143, 150-151, 159-166, 171, 173-175, 179-180, 183, 189, 196
circle dancing, 50, 171, 173
clairvoyance, 15-16, 83
Clay-Egerton, Alastair, 175,
Clay-Egerton, Meriem, 32, 112, 122, 194
clearings, 4, 30, 89, 103, 105, 111, 166, 190, 192
cliffs, 55, 81-82, 89
climate, 172
clothes, 140, 172-174
clouds, 60, 86, 124, 144, 190
clover, 106, 125
clumps, 3-4, 23, 38, 40, 42, 50, 55, 61, 94
Cochrane, Robert, 55, 76, 194
coincidence, 99
Collins, Andrew, 105, 174, 194-195
composers, 24
computer network, 91
Cone of Power, 174-175
consciousness, 5, 11, 14-15, 24, 32, 36, 90, 93, 103, 122, 136-137, 143, 146-147, 194
conservation, 160

Constable, Trevor James, 174-175, 194
Cornwall, 53, 73
cosmic consciousness, 5, 14-15, 93, 194
covens, 50, 76, 151, 169
Cries, 155, 168-169
crop circles, 161, 178
Crowley, Vivianne, 27, 194
Crowther, Patricia, 168-169, 194
crystals, 184
Cunningham, Scott, 136, 194
cuttings, 62, 111
Cypress, 138

dancing, 50, 61, 75, 119, 147, 158, 160, 171, 173-176
danger, 115
dangers, 115
Dark of the Moon, 144-145, 183
dawn, 44, 80, 142, 144
death, 116, 165, 185
deer, 124, 161
deer paths, 161
deserts, 20-21
Devereux, Paul, 2, 63, 97, 147, 154, 194
Devil's Cave, 56
Devil's Pulpit, 61
Dew, 50, 74, 77
dew pond, 50, 74
dewponds, 23, 74-75, 77
Diana of the Tree Ways, 87
Diana's Mirror, 76
Diana Trivia, 87
Dickinson, Bob, 61, 69, 71, 143, 194
Dingley Dell, 47
disabilities, 115, 175
disorientation, 19, 31, 35
dowsing, 18, 20, 74, 101-102, 120

199

Dozmary Pool, 73
Dragon Hill, 125
Dragon Project, 125
Drawing Down the Moon, 19, 76
dreams, 36, 88, 90, 98-99, 149, 155
Druids, 5, 38, 126
drumming, 147
dryads, 20
dusk, 48, 144-147, 151, 155

echo, 3, 12, 87, 142, 170, 179
echoes, 35, 53, 98, 142, 169, 179
elder, 3, 38, 62, 68, 74, 113, 157, 159
Elder Mother, 68
elemental beings, 94, 145, 149-150, 163
elements, 0, 23, 29, 34, 79, 82, 88-90, 121, 144, 154, 167, 195
Elgar, Edward, 24-25, 196
Ellis, Robin, 30, 32, 36, 195
Elm, 9-10, 38, 196
essential oils, 136

Fairies, 22, 63, 70
fairy ring, 161
Fairy Stones, 22
fasting, 101, 147
fear, 80, 115-116, 150, 176
feast, 109, 140, 172
Feeling, 5, 7, 15, 19, 33, 36, 43, 48, 50, 53, 59, 68, 71, 81-82, 95-96, 107, 109, 133-134, 140, 149, 153, 157, 159, 163, 168, 173, 176, 182, 185, 188-189, 192
festivals, 43, 109, 118, 166, 173
Field corners, 50-51

fields, 4, 20, 50-51, 61, 69, 75, 89, 95, 106, 111, 118, 120, 124, 139, 165, 176, 178
Fire, 29, 43, 55, 59-60, 79, 82, 85-86, 137, 173
Fire of Azrael, 82, 137
five-lanes ends, 87
flowers, 10, 77, 81, 89, 159, 163, 183-184
folklore, 22, 51, 75, 196
forest, 16-17, 29-32, 36-37, 40, 42, 62, 88-89, 95, 103, 141, 147, 172, 178, 187, 192, 195
Fortune, Dion, 25, 53, 55, 82, 137, 195
Fox, George, 135
Frazer, James, 76, 195
Friends of the Earth, 5
fruits, 81, 183
Full Moon, 12, 22, 36, 61, 76-77, 82-83, 86, 106, 111, 118, 129, 141, 145-147, 174
fungi, 38, 136, 161

Gardner, Gerald, 30, 149, 168, 172, 187, 195
garlands, 166, 179, 183, 188
Gateways, 74, 118, 129
Genius Loci, 13
geography, 16, 21, 23, 88
ghosts, 22, 51, 115
Gill's Lap, 40, 141
Giving and Taking, 0, 184
Glastonbury, 85, 97
Goddard, Jimmy, 40, 142, 195
Golding, Lawrence, 159, 195
goose fat, 172
gorse, 4, 42, 94
grain, 183

grasses, 4, 10, 37, 42, 89, 94, 111, 118-119, 125, 128, 132-133, 141, 161, 184
Graves, 26, 77, 143, 195
Greece, 23
green flash, 145
Green, Marian, 5, 10, 35, 42, 69-70, 89, 96, 108-109, 126, 128-129, 145, 165, 183, 185, 193, 195, 197
green spirituality, 5
ground, 4, 23, 33, 47-48, 68-69, 86, 89, 95, 105, 107-108, 112, 122, 125-126, 133-134, 136, 139-141, 160, 164, 166, 176, 181, 183
ground surface, 160
groves, 11-12, 25, 37-41, 45, 47-48, 56, 89, 126, 137, 139, 143, 166, 183
guardians, 48, 68, 118, 124, 126, 156, 158, 160, 196
Haegtessa, 50
hair, 26, 79, 142
Hallowe'en, 118, 196
hallucination, 172
Hardy, Thomas, 24,
hares, 120, 122, 124
Hare paths, 120, 122
Harte, Jeremy, 51, 195
harvest loaf, 184
hawthorn, 4, 37, 66, 68, 74, 89, 111, 118, 128, 165-166, 178, 180
haymaking, 50
Hazel, 32, 37, 62, 101, 182
head-hum, 19
healing, 7, 24, 66, 94, 97, 136, 159
heaths, 49, 116
Hecate, 87
hedge dating, 51

Hedge Rider, 50
Hedge Sitter, 50
hedges, 4, 49-51, 111
Helen's Well, 64, 68
Hidden Company, 151, 192
Hiley, Denise, 37, 56, 195
hills, 17, 25, 57, 65, 76, 84-86, 90, 98, 108, 118, 124, 196
hilltops, 23, 40, 84-85, 165
Hinduism, 11
hollows, 4, 44, 55, 57, 59-60, 66, 70, 90, 124
holly, 37-38, 48, 85, 89, 118, 123, 129
Holy Wells, 66, 156, 158, 194, 197
honeysuckle, 135, 138, 183
Hopkins, R. Thurston, 43, 195
Hornbeam, 38
Howard, Mike, 2, 193
hydrological cycle, 65
Hyssop, 138

Ice Age, 60
imagination, 77, 88, 145, 150, 175
Imbolc, 118, 195
incense, 60, 83, 137, 147, 188
India, 21
Iris, 138
iron, 179
Ivy, 38, 89

Jackson, Nigel Aldcroft, 50, 195
Jones, Evan John, 151, 189, 192, 195-196
juniper, 83, 138

kahunas, 21, 100-101
Keats, 135
Kent, 30, 40, 42, 58, 108, 139, 195

201

knives, 33, 122, 182, 189
Koppana, Kati-Ma, 31, 195
kundalini, 110

Lady in White, 75
Lady of the Lake, 73
Lake District, 17
Lake Poets, 24
lakes, 17, 65, 90
Lammas, 118, 150, 161, 166, 185
landscape aesthetics, 109
landscape, 5, 8-10, 13, 16, 18, 20-25, 29, 59, 65, 85-91, 98-99, 105, 109, 120-121, 124, 131, 138, 144-145, 155-156, 160-161, 163-167, 177, 191-194
Langstone, Alex, 70, 195
language, 170, 176
larch, 32-33, 38
Laws of Manifestation, 99
leaves, 10, 36, 45, 60, 68, 79, 87, 112, 118, 147, 155, 159, 163, 165-166, 173, 183-184
legend, 22, 43, 56, 59-61, 66, 73-74, 125, 197
Leland, Charles Godfrey, 172, 195
Lethbridge, T. C., 20-22, 70, 195
leys, 40, 121
Liddell, W. E., 186, 195
light, 36, 49, 59, 79, 81-82, 85, 89, 120, 144-146, 150-151, 171, 183, 187, 190, 197
Lilac, 138
Lily of the Valley, 138
Lincolnshire, 24, 60, 161, 196
litter, 157
Lourdes, 24
Lud's Cave, 56
Lud's Church, 56

Lud's Well, 69, 194
Lughnasadh, 118
Lydford Gorge, 70

Mabey, Richard, 110, 195
magic circle, 51, 161, 164
magic, 3, 43-44, 51, 59, 71, 73, 99, 139, 145, 149, 161, 164, 171, 178, 189, 195-197
Magical Aromatherapy, 136, 194
magical orders, 147
magical tools, 179, 181
Malvern Hills, 25, 141
mana, 21
maps, 98-99, 101, 164
Mason, Stanley Weston, 85
massage, 136, 142, 158
Matthews, John, 84, 196
May Day, 43, 77
May Eve, 118, 161, 166, 196
mazes, 85, 117, 119, 175
Meadowsweet, 138
meditation, 6-7, 9, 36, 46, 48, 88-89, 97-98, 109, 147, 149, 155, 171
memory, 3-4, 34-35, 40, 77, 84, 97, 99, 112, 120, 126, 179, 194
Mesmer, Anton, 21
metal, 179
Michell, John, 8, 17, 21-22, 121, 125, 196
midnight, 12, 22, 43, 59, 61, 74-75, 77, 106, 110, 141-142, 145, 147, 174, 183
Midsummer Day, 141
Midsummer Hill, 141
Milne, A. A., 42, 141, 196
mint, 172
moon-dew, 77
Moon Goddess, 61, 83, 87

Moon, 7, 12, 19, 22, 36, 61, 71, 73, 75-77, 82-83, 86-87, 96, 100, 106, 111, 118, 129, 141, 144-147, 155, 164-165, 174, 176, 183, 187, 190
moonlight, 33, 77, 86, 145-146, 183
Moonraker, 76
moorlands, 20
morphogenetic fields, 124
Morris, William, 9, 196
mounds, 23, 85
mountain-tops, 84
mountains, 17, 20-21, 57, 65, 178
Movement, 132, 155, 171, 175-176, 191, 193
Mugwort, 138
munia, 21
Murray, Margaret, 49, 196
music, 12, 25, 83, 142-143, 168
Mystery Traditions, 121
mythology, 20

naiads, 20
Naked Man, 88
names, 14, 40, 59, 98, 118-119, 138, 169
National Parks, 17
nature spirits, 19, 36, 49, 63, 125, 144-145, 149, 151, 175, 196
necklaces, 183
Neolithic, 179
nereids, 20
nettles, 69, 122, 133, 141, 152, 157, 160, 173
Nevern, 124
New Forest, 17, 30, 88, 172, 187
New Moon, 100, 144-145
Nicholson, John, 196

night, 32-33, 44, 62, 77, 83, 86, 90, 111, 129, 131, 135, 137, 141, 144, 164, 168, 176, 187, 190
No Man's Land, 51
Northern Tradition, 21, 147, 196
Northumberland, 73, 129
Norway, 116
nudity, 44, 88, 140, 171-173, 175, 178
nymphs, 20

oak, 4, 7, 10, 30, 32, 37-38, 60, 88-89, 92, 94-95, 124, 183
oakwood, 165
oats, 185
Odin, 155
odyle, 21
Old Religion, 37, 42, 59, 61, 193
olive oil, 172
oreads, 20
orgasm, 177
orgone, 21, 74-75
Otherworld, 18, 31, 36, 48, 50, 88, 122, 128, 144-145, 147
out-of-the-body experience, 90
owls, 12, 124
Oxfordshire, 125
oxygen, 29

Padfield, Tony, 120, 122, 196
Pagan Federation, 193
painter, 144
painting, 144
Pan, 25, 103
parish boundaries, 51
paths, 16, 18, 26, 30-31, 37, 44, 48-49, 62, 83, 85, 87, 89, 102, 106-107, 112, 119-122, 126, 128, 133, 135, 161, 197

203

paths, 10, 25, 31, 33-35, 84, 86-88, 107-108, 120-122, 126
pathworking, 88-89, 93, 155
Pembrokeshire, 124
Pennick, Nigel, 2, 13, 147, 196
Pennines, 53
perfume, 135-136
perfumer, 136
Phillips, Guy Raglan, 126, 141, 178, 186, 196
picnics, 7, 108-109, 139, 160, 195
pilgrimage, 24, 118-119
Pine, 38, 40, 47, 61, 90, 94, 124, 135, 137-138, 143, 196
pissing, 109, 163
planting, 48, 160
plastic, 68, 179, 183
poetry, 24, 26, 137, 192
ponds, 30, 50, 74-77, 79, 85
pools, 22, 68, 70, 73-74, 79-80, 89, 129, 146, 159, 184, 195
poppies, 165
Powys, John, 24, 119, 122
prana, 21
primaeval forests, 36, 116
Privet, 40
Psyche, 134, 146
psychic ability, 96, 105
psychic phenomena, 15
Psychic Questing, 105
psychic sense, 19, 146-147
psychic traces, 87
psychoactive plants, 147

Quakerism, 186

rags, 69
railway lines, 111
railways, 62, 103, 111-112, 115
rain, 2, 59, 65, 73, 120, 135-137, 155, 167-168, 181

Raven, Morgan, 149, 196
rebirth, 116, 165, 185, 197
Reich, 21
Reichenbach, Karl von, 21
resins, 136-137
Richardson, Alan, 25,
Richardson, Janian, 62, 70, 196
Rider, 50, 195-196
Ritual nudity, 171-172
ritual tools, 179, 181
rituals, 10-11, 30, 36-37, 39, 43, 50, 55-59, 63, 82, 100, 107, 109, 111, 118, 121-122, 125, 140-141, 144, 148-150, 154-155, 157, 159-164, 166-167, 171-175, 161, 163, 166, 173, 183-185, 186-189
rivers, 25, 65, 111
roads, 86-88, 115, 195
robes, 172, 174
rock outcrops, 17, 23, 62
rock, 4, 16-17, 23, 31, 52-53, 55-57, 60-62, 70-71, 89, 121, 124, 147, 177, 181, 184, 197
Roe deer, 161
Rose, 33, 57, 120, 138
rowan, 10, 89, 129
Rudkin, Ethel, 75, 196
runes, 155
Ryall, Rhiannon, 76, 196
Sacred Groves, 38, 37-38, 40, 47-48, 56, 143, 156
Samhain, 118
sandalwood, 83
Scent, 37, 60, 81, 83, 134-138, 174, 176
Scotland, 145
Scots Pine, 38, 40, 143
scrying, 76-77, 146
Scunthorpe, 59
sea, 20-21, 25, 55, 73, 80, 82-83, 89-90, 129, 142, 145, 195

204

Seashore, 0, 80-83
seaside, 65, 80
seasons, 35, 97, 116, 118, 120, 131, 140, 144, 165, 179
secrets, 35-36, 149, 156
Selene, 103, 196
sex, 177-178
sexual ecstasy, 147
sexual feelings, 109, 177
shamanic journeying, 88, 90
shamans, 16
Sheldrake, Rupert, 124, 196
Silent Pool, 73-74
Simons, Paul, 29, 196
simulacra, 124, 196
sitting out, 93, 147-148, 171
skin, 140, 157, 169, 172-173
Sky, 3, 7, 10, 32, 42, 48, 50, 56-57, 82, 85, 112, 118, 144-145, 164, 167, 190
skyclad, 12, 140, 167, 171-173
Smith, Jill, 43, 45
snow, 155, 165-166
soil, 16, 43, 53
sound, 29, 66, 71, 74, 80, 83, 118, 132-134, 142-143, 147, 163, 176
sounds, 25, 32, 35, 71, 75, 81, 132-133, 142-144, 169, 196
spices, 136-137
spine, 44, 70, 109
springs, 10-12, 24, 30, 45, 60, 66, 68, 73, 89, 114, 122, 128, 132, 138, 147-148, 158-159, 177, 185, 194, 196
Spurn Point, 82
standing stones, 23, 85
stangs, 183, 188
Star Exercise, 174-175
starlight, 33
stiles, 30

stone circles, 23, 85
Stonehenge, 97
stones, 16, 22-23, 27, 70, 85, 133-134, 141, 143, 160, 173, 176, 184
streams, 20-21, 65, 70, 98
Subtle Geography, 16
Sufis, 175-176
summer, 10, 17, 106, 129, 137, 144-145, 161, 194-195
Sun, 43, 48-49, 65, 85, 89, 118, 129, 144-146, 151, 160, 164-165, 171, 178
sunlight, 33, 75, 79, 105
sunrise, 85
sunset, 85, 111, 145, 186, 188, 195
Surrey, 50, 73, 195
Sussex, 40, 42-43, 53, 83, 86, 88, 195
Sycamore, 38
Symes, Keith, 10, 196
synchronicity, 99, 105

Taoism, 8, 11, 87, 121
Taplin, Kim, 26, 119, 197
Taste, 119, 139
Taylor, Ian, 59, 66, 74-75, 158, 197
telepathy, 15
temples, 10, 84, 196
tending, 38, 149, 155-158
thickets, 8, 30, 85
thorn, 3, 68-69, 122-124
thorns, 104, 128, 141, 173
tides, 25, 73, 80
times, 4, 12, 18, 21-23, 26-27, 31-32, 43, 52, 55-56, 59-61, 63, 66, 95, 97, 106-107, 111, 116, 118, 120, 133-134, 137, 144, 159, 164-166, 169, 171, 173, 179, 183, 185, 187-188

205

tingling, 19, 109
Tools, 179, 181, 183
touch, 16, 81, 141, 157, 164, 178, 193, 196
tracks, 23, 74, 86-88, 90, 121
traditional witchcraft, 1, 13, 30, 84, 87, 186-187
trance, 23, 149, 173, 175-176
tree calendar, 40
tree clumps, 40, 50
tree spirits, 34
tree trunk, 125, 181, 184
Trees, 4, 10, 16-17, 20-21, 27, 29, 31-32, 34-35, 37-38, 40, 42-45, 47-49, 53, 56, 60, 62, 68-69, 71, 74, 79, 88- 90, 92, 94-95, 103-104, 106-109, 111-112, 118, 122, 124, 126, 128-129, 132, 136-139, 142-143, 157, 159, 163, 165-166, 176, 185, 190, 197
trespassing, 116, 158
triple Goddess, 174
twigs, 29, 141, 147, 155, 163, 173

undergrowth, 25, 31, 33, 35, 142
Universalist, 186
unofficial countryside, 7, 110, 195
Valiente, Doreen, 42-43, 50, 59, 76, 83-84, 86, 88, 96, 142-143, 171, 174, 193, 195, 197
vapours, 23, 83
vervain, 172
Virgin Mary, 24
visions, 83
visual impairment, 115
visualisation, 160

walking meditation, 48, 171
wands, 105, 179, 182-183, 185, 188
wasteland, 95

water spirits, 66
water, 12, 29, 57, 65-66, 68, 70-71, 73-77, 79-80, 82-83, 100, 102, 108, 124, 129, 132, 143, 146, 150, 158-159, 181, 183, 188, 195-197
waterfalls, 17, 20-21, 55, 57, 69-70, 73, 97, 142, 177
Watkins, Alfred, 38, 40
Watkins, Allen, 121
Watkins, Kay, 45, 94, 157
Watts, 16
waves, 73, 80-81, 83, 110, 122, 142
weather, 29, 59, 82, 136, 138, 140, 155, 167
Wedd, 38, 40, 100, 139, 197
Westmorland, 186
wheat, 118, 178, 185
Wheel of the Year, 165
Whelan, 2, 66, 158, 197
White Lady waterfall, 70
White Lady, 70, 75, 195
willow, 10, 40, 124
Wilson, 56, 197
Wiltshire, 38
Wilverley Post, 88
wind, 3, 12, 29, 31, 33, 40, 44, 55, 59-60, 75, 82, 86, 102, 118, 132-133, 136, 142-143, 147, 155, 165, 167, 169, 173, 178
wine, 9, 76, 188-189
winter, 29, 60-61, 75, 144, 166, 185, 194, 196-197
witchcraft, 5, 27, 30, 50, 84, 100, 163, 171-172, 175, 186-187, 195, 197
witches' meeting places, 161
witches, 30, 49-50, 61, 77, 84, 86-88, 110, 140, 156, 161, 170-172, 174-175, 186-187, 192, 194-195

206

Women, 115, 121, 124
Worcestershire, 3, 62, 196
Words, 7-8, 12, 16, 19, 21, 55, 68, 90, 96, 135, 140, 148, 157-158, 168-170, 176, 179, 187, 192
Working Tools, 0, 179, 181, 183
worship, 27, 56, 59, 149, 174
wouivre, 21
writers, 1, 21, 24, 35
Wych Cross, 88
Wye Valley, 17

Yarrow, 138
year, 62, 97, 116, 118, 120-121, 131, 135, 138, 155, 164-167, 172, 178, 182
yew, 25-26, 38, 48, 69, 124
yogis, 21
Yorkshire, 60, 77, 82, 125, 159, 196-197
Yule, 118

Zen, 11

Other titles from Capall Bann

A detailed illustrated catalogue is available on request, SAE or International Postal Coupon appreciated. Titles are available direct from Capall Bann, post free in the UK (cheque or PO with order) or from good bookshops and specialist outlets.

Animals, Mind Body Spirit & Folklore
Angels and Goddesses - Celtic Christianity & Paganism by Michael Howard
Arthur - The Legend Unveiled by C Johnson & E Lung
Auguries and Omens - The Magical Lore of Birds by Yvonne Aburrow
Book of the Veil The by Peter Paddon
Call of the Horned Piper by Nigel Jackson
Cats' Company by Ann Walker
Celtic Lore & Druidic Ritual by Rhiannon Ryall
Compleat Vampyre - The Vampyre Shaman: Werewolves & Witchery by Nigel Jackson
Crystal Clear - A Guide to Quartz Crystal by Jennifer Dent
Earth Dance - A Year of Pagan Rituals by Jan Brodie

Earth Magic by Margaret McArthur
Enchanted Forest - The Magical Lore of Trees by Yvonne Aburrow
Healing Homes by Jennifer Dent
Herbcraft - Shamanic & Ritual Use of Herbs by Susan Lavender & Anna Franklin
In Search of Herne the Hunter by Eric Fitch
Inner Space Workbook - Developing Counselling & Magical Skills Through the Tarot
Kecks, Keddles & Kesh by Michael Bayley
Living Tarot by Ann Walker
Magical Incenses and Perfumes by Jan Brodie
Magical Lore of Animals by Yvonne Aburrow
Magical Lore of Cats by Marion Davies

Magical Lore of Herbs by Marion Davies
Masks of Misrule - The Horned God & His Cult in Europe by Nigel Jackson
Mysteries of the Runes by Michael Howard
Oracle of Geomancy by Nigel Pennick
Patchwork of Magic by Julia Day
Pathworking - A Practical Book of Guided Meditations by Pete Jennings
Pickingill Papers - The Origins of Gardnerian Wicca by Michael Howard
Psychic Animals by Dennis Bardens
Psychic Self Defence - Real Solutions by Jan Brodie
Runic Astrology by Nigel Pennick
Sacred Animals by Gordon 'The Toad' Maclellan
Sacred Grove - The Mysteries of the Forest by Yvonne Aburrow
Sacred Geometry by Nigel Pennick
Sacred Lore of Horses The by Marion Davies
Sacred Ring - Pagan Origins British Folk Festivals & Customs by Michael Howard
Secret Places of the Goddess by Philip Heselton
Talking to the Earth by Gordon Maclellan
Taming the Wolf - Full Moon Meditations by Steve Hounsome
The Goddess Year by Nigel Pennick & Helen Field
West Country Wicca by Rhiannon Ryall
Wildwood King by Philip Kane
Witches of Oz The by Matthew & Julia Phillips

Capall Bann is owned and run by people actively involved in many of the areas in which we publish. Our list is expanding rapidly so do contact us for details on the latest releases. We guarantee our mailing list will never be released to other companies or organisations.

Capall Bann Publishing, Freshfields, Chieveley, Berks, RG20 8TF.